24ᵗʰ February 2019

THE HABIT OF HOLINESS

To Sadie,

With prayers on the
occasion of your
&
Confirmation,

From all at
St Michael & All
Angels,
Bedford Park

G000278691

THE HABIT OF HOLINESS

DAILY PRAYER

COMPILED BY

MARTIN WARNER

CANON PASTOR, ST PAUL'S CATHEDRAL

morehouse

Continuum
The Tower Building
11 York Road
London SE1 7NX

Continuum
15 East 26th Street
New York
NY 10010

Morehouse
4775 Linglestown Road
Harrisburg
PA 17112

Morehouse in an imprint of Continuum Books

www.continuumbooks.com

First published 2004

British Library Cataloguing-in-Publication Data
A catalogue record for this book is available from the British Library.

ISBN 0819281409

Designed and typeset by Tony Chung and Benn Linfield.
Printed and bound by MPG Books, Cornwall.

CONTENTS

INTRODUCTION

A book to inhabit
This is a book to inhabit, one of those items, like a watch, keys, or mobile phone, that you have with you. A poignant and true story perhaps illustrates what this inhabiting might mean.

An English family (mother, father and two young teenagers) are on holiday in Tuscany. Without warning, father collapses in the street; a fatal heart attack. Numb with shock, as the crowd gathers and the ambulance is sent for, mother takes from her husband's jacket pocket the prayer book he was never without. She kneels and reads aloud his daily prayer: the General Thanksgiving. The children never forgot the comfort of that moment.

The importance of a daily routine of prayer becomes apparent in exceptional circumstances when we want to stretch out and catch heaven by the hems. It is then that the strand of routine prayer can bind and strengthen, revealing its hidden transforming power.

There is no right or wrong way to inhabit this book; how you use it should feel as comfortable and unique as your own home. Habits of prayer are for you to design, in ways that fit your life. This book may be a helpful resource in that process; a person whose advice you value can also be important in helping to shape your habit.

About this book
This collection of prayers was inspired by *The Treasury of Devotion*, first published in 1869, and unattributed prayers are generally drawn from that source. This book seeks to provide prayers to accompany you throughout the day, the week, the year, your life.

The headings are not intended to be prescriptive or rigid, but a guide for how your day or week might be irrigated by the grace of prayer. Sometimes more than one prayer is offered in a particular category; be confident about choosing as little or as much as suits your needs.

This book can also be a channel of grace to carry you into other ways of deepening your interior life with God: pondering the scriptures, sharing in the Eucharist, vocation to a particular ministry, or sharing in a fuller version of the daily Office (Morning and Evening Prayer).

For the most part, the context of these devotions is envisaged as personal and individual. Occasionally they imply reference to priestly ministry.

Clothed in Christ

Inhabiting the world of holiness into which this book gazes, and shaping your own habit of prayer; these actions are a symbol; a form of dress – a fashion statement.

Inhabiting this book is a means to that end, the fashioning of your life on that of Christ:

> For all of you are the children of God, through faith, in Christ Jesus, since everyone of you that has been baptised has been clothed in Christ.
>
> (Galatians 3:28)

 1 PRAYER AND TEACHING

Now it happened that Jesus was in a certain place praying, and when he had finished one of his disciples said, 'Lord, teach us to pray, as John taught his disciples.'

(Luke 11:1)

Prayer and teaching are different aspects of the same activity.

Jesus inspires a desire to pray through his own example of praying, thereby prompting the disciple to inquire further into the mystery of this aspect of their master's life. Example can be the gift of instruction we offer to others.

The following prayers are common forms in Christian devotion and liturgy. They are a well-used gift from countless generations, and it is good to know them by heart.

Weave them into the fabric of your life, so that they grow in richness through association with important moments, places, and people in your life. And let them become the material with which you in turn inspire and teach others to pray.

Foundations of Christian Devotion

The Apostles' Creed
I believe in God, the Father almighty, maker of heaven and earth.
And in Jesus Christ, his only Son, our Lord,
who was conceived by the Holy Ghost, born of the Virgin Mary,
suffered under Pontius Pilate, was crucified, dead, and buried.
He descended into hell; the third day he rose again from the dead;
he ascended into heaven, and sitteth at the right hand of God, the
Father almighty;
from thence he shall come to judge the quick and the dead.
I believe in the Holy Ghost; the Holy Catholic Church;
the Communion of Saints; the forgiveness of sins;
the resurrection of the body; and the life everlasting
Amen.

The Lord's Prayer
Our Father,
who art in heaven,
hallowed be thy name;
thy kingdom come;
thy will be done;
on earth as it is in heaven.
Give us this day our daily bread.
And forgive us our trespasses,
as we forgive those who trespass against us.
And lead us not into temptation;
but deliver us from evil.
For thine is the kingdom,
the power and the glory
for ever and ever.
Amen.

or

Our Father in heaven,
hallowed be your name,
your kingdom come,
your will be done,
on earth as in heaven.
Give us today our daily bread.
Forgive us our sins
as we forgive those who sin against us.
Lead us not into temptation
but deliver us from evil.
For the kingdom, the power,
and the glory are yours
now and for ever.
Amen.

The 'Glory be'

Glory be to the Father, and to the Son, and to the Holy Spirit;
as it was in the beginning, is now, and ever shall be, world
without end. *Amen.*

or

Glory to the Father and to the Son and to the Holy Spirit;
as it was in the beginning is now and shall be for ever. *Amen.*

The 'Hail Mary'

Hail Mary, full of grace, the Lord is with thee. Blessed art thou
among women, and blessed is the fruit of thy womb, Jesus.
Holy Mary, mother of God, pray for us sinners now, and at the
hour of our death.
Amen.

The Angelus
(*Traditionally said each morning and evening, and at noon.*)
The Angel of the Lord brought tidings to Mary;
> And she conceived by the Holy Spirit.   Hail Mary …

Behold the handmaid of the Lord;
> Be it unto me according to your word.   Hail Mary …

And the Word was made flesh;
> And dwelt among us.   Hail Mary …

Pray for us, O holy Mother of God;
> That we may be made worthy of the promises of Christ.

Let us pray.
We beseech you, O Lord, pour your grace into our hearts, that as we have known the incarnation of your Son, Jesus Christ, by the message of an angel, so by his + cross and passion we may be brought to the glory of his resurrection; through the same Christ our Lord. *Amen.*

In Eastertide the Regina coeli *may be said instead.*
Joy to thee, O Queen of heaven, alleluia!
He whom thou wast meet to bear, alleluia!
As he promised has arisen, alleluia!
Pour for us to God thy prayer, alleluia!

Rejoice and be glad O Virgin Mary, alleluia!
> For the Lord is risen indeed, alleluia!

Let us pray
O God, who by the resurrection of your Son, our Lord Jesus Christ, has given joy to all creation; may we, aided by the prayers of Mary, his Mother, obtain the joy of everlasting life. We ask this through Christ the Lord. *Amen.*

Foundations of Christian Instruction

The Ten Commandments

1 God spoke all these words and said: I am the Lord your God, who brought you out of the land of Egypt, out of the house of slavery; you shall have no other gods before me.
2 You shall not make for yourself an idol, whether in the form of anything that is in heaven above, or that is on the earth beneath, or that is in the water under the earth. You shall not bow down to them or worship them.
3 You shall not make wrongful use of the name of the Lord your God.
4 Remember the Sabbath day, and keep it holy.
5 Honour your father and mother.
6 You shall not murder.
7 You shall not commit adultery.
8 You shall not steal.
9 You shall not bear false witness.
10 You shall not covet your neighbour's house; you shall not covet your neighbour's wife, or male or female slave, or ox, or donkey, or anything that belongs to your neighbour.

The Habits of Christian Life

1 To observe the festivals and holy-days appointed.
2 To keep fast-days with devotion.
3 To observe the customs and ceremonies established.
4 To pray the offices of Matins and Evensong, if time and appropriate circumstance permit.
5 To receive the blessed sacrament of the body and blood of Christ with frequent devotion, and three times a year at least, of which Easter is always to be one. And for the better preparation thereof, to unburden and quieten our consciences of those sins that may grieve us, or scruples that may trouble us, to a wise and godly priest, and from him receive advice and the benefit of absolution. *(After Bishop Cosin)*

The Sacraments
1 Baptism.
2 The Eucharist.
3 Confirmation.
4 Penance.
5 Ordination.
6 Matrimony.
7 Anointing of the sick.

The Theological Virtues
1 Faith.
2 Hope.
3 Charity.

The Cardinal Virtues
1 Justice.
2 Prudence.
3 Temperance.
4 Fortitude.

The Gifts of the Holy Spirit
1 Wisdom.
2 Understanding.
3 Counsel.
4 Inward strength.
5 Knowledge.
6 True godliness.
7 Holy fear.

(from Isaiah 11:2-3)

The Fruits of the Holy Spirit

1　Love.

2　Joy.

3　Peace.

4　Long-suffering.

5　Gentleness.

6　Goodness.

7　Faith.

8　Meekness.

9　Patience.

10　Modesty.

11　Temperance.

12　Chastity.

(from Galatians 5.22)

The Spiritual Works of Mercy

1　To instruct the ignorant.

2　To correct offenders.

3　To counsel doubters.

4　To comfort the afflicted.

5　To suffer injuries with patience.

6　To forgive offences and wrongs.

7　To pray for others.

The Corporal Works of Mercy

1　To feed the hungry and give drink to the thirsty.

2　To clothe the naked.

3　To give shelter to the stranger and needy.

4　To visit the sick.

5　To minister to captives and prisoners.

6　To visit the fatherless and widows.

7　To bury the dead.

(from Matthew 25:31-46)

Prayer and Teaching

The Beatitudes

1 Blessed are the poor in spirit, for theirs is the kingdom of heaven.
2 Blessed are those who mourn, for they will be comforted.
3 Blessed are the meek, for they shall inherit the earth.
4 Blessed are those who hunger and thirst for righteousness, for they will be filled.
5 Blessed are the merciful, for they shall obtain mercy.
6 Blessed are the pure in heart, for they will see God.
7 Blessed are the peacemakers, for they will be called children of God.
8 Blessed are those who are persecuted for righteousness' sake, for theirs is the kingdom of heaven.

(from Matthew 5:3-11)

The Deadly Sins and their Contrary Virtues

1 Pride.	1 Humility.
2 Covetousness.	2 Generosity.
3 Lust.	3 Chastity.
4 Envy.	4 Gentleness.
5 Gluttony.	5 Temperance.
6 Anger.	6 Patience.
7 Sloth.	7 Diligence.

Ways of Participating in Another's Sin

1 By counsel.
2 By command.
3 By consent.
4 By provocation.
5 By praise or flattery.
6 By concealment.
7 By partaking.
8 By silence.
9 By defence of wrong.

Sins against the Holy Spirit

1 Presuming on God's mercy.
2 Despair.
3 Calling into question a known truth.
4 Envy at another's good.
5 Obstinacy in sin.
6 Final impenitence.

Notable Duties

1 Prayer.
2 Fasting.
3 Almsgiving.

The Parts of True Repentance

1 Contrition (sorrow for sin and resolve not to sin again).
2 Confession (the individual articulation before God of sin and repentance).
3 Satisfaction (the consequent amendment of life, in prayer and action).

The Penitential Psalms

Psalms 6, 32, 38, 51, 102, 130, 143.

The Gradual Psalms

Psalms 120 to 134.

The Evangelical Counsels

1 Voluntary poverty.
2 Perpetual chastity.
3 Holy obedience.

The Seven Words from the Cross

1 Father, forgive them, for they know not what they do. (Luke 23:34)
2 Truly, I say to you that today you will be with me in paradise.

(Luke 23:43)

3 Woman, behold your son!...Behold, your mother! (John 19.26, 27)
4 My God, my God, why hast thou forsaken me? (Matthew 27:46)
5 I thirst. (John 19:28)
6 It is finished. (John 19:30)
7 Father, into your hands I commend my spirit. (Luke 23:46)

The Four Last Things

1 Death.
2 Judgement.
3 Heaven.
4 Hell.

An Exhortation

Remember, Christian soul, that on this and every day you have

God to glorify
Jesus to imitate
A soul to save
A body to honour
Sins to repent of
Virtues to practise
Hell to shun
Heaven to gain
Eternity to prepare for
Time to profit by
Neighbours to serve
The world to transform
Creation to enjoy
Evil to combat
Temptations to overcome
Death, perhaps, to suffer
Judgement to undergo
And in all things thanks to render
to the God in whose image you were made.

DAILY DEVOTIONS

Devotion is the offering of your love to God. Christian life without devotion is like a relationship of unrequited love.

Devotion has a variety of forms. You are the one to design the style and extent of your response to God (making a Rule of Life), so that it is the measure and expression of you, your life and love.

The pattern of daily devotions offered here suggests a framework for that expression at the beginning and end of each day. There are also prayers that label very ordinary daily actions, and an outline of devotions that might be used at any time, either at home, or as the basis for a visit to church in order to pray.

These prayers said and done can usefully be described as 'the practice' of your religion. Their determined, practical routine (no harm in that) can both fit and also shape the contours of your life, irrespective of shifting mood and inclination.

But they are also the rehearsal, preparing you at every level of existence for the vision of God. Prayer (more than prayers) is the aptitude for that vision, the symptom of your vocation to holiness and perfection.

OCCASIONAL MORNING PRAYERS

Glory be to the Father, who created me.
Glory be to the Son, who redeemed me.
Glory be to the Holy Spirit, who sanctifies me.
Blessed be the Holy Trinity, now and for evermore,
I consecrate this day entirely to your love and to your greater glory.
I know not what this day shall bring forth, either pleasant or troublous;
whether I shall be happy or sorrowful, shall enjoy consolation
or undergo pain and grief; it shall be as you please.
I give myself into your hands and submit to whatever you will. *Amen*.

(St Francis Xavier)

Work, O Lord, thy holy will in me and by me this day.
Protect me, guide me, bless me,
that I may do something today for love of thee;
something to please thee, so that this evening I may be nearer to thee,
though I see it not, nor know it.
Lead me, good Jesus, to thyself,
and keep me in thy grace unto the end,
that with thy saints I may praise thee for ever and ever. *Amen.*

(Edward Pusey)

O eternal God, you have made all things for us, as you have made us
for your glory; sanctify my body and soul, my thoughts and my
intentions, my words and actions, that whatsoever I shall think, or
speak, or do, may be by me designed to the glorification of your
Name; that doing all things for your glory here, I may be partaker
of your glory hereafter, through Jesus Christ our Lord. *Amen.*

(Jeremy Taylor)

+ The power of the Father govern and protect me!
The wisdom of the Son teach and enlighten me!
The influence of the Holy Spirit enliven and renew me!
And the blessing of the everlasting and All-Holy Trinity
be with me, with those I love, and those I meet,
this day and evermore. *Amen.*

A Dedication of the Day

O God, I firmly believe that you are present here;
perfectly seeing me, you observe all my actions and
know all my thoughts.

Keep a moment's silence as you place yourself consciously before God
and in union with saints, angels and Christians who begin this day with you.

I praise and thank you from my inmost heart,
for you have created me in your own image,
redeemed me with the precious blood of your dear Son,
and brought me to the beginning of this new day;
I dedicate in return my body and soul, with all their powers and faculties,
and all the thoughts, words, and actions of this day;

To your eternal protection and mercy I commend
all those for whom I ought to pray... :
supply their needs and support them in all their troubles,
deliver them in their temptations and dangers,
guide them through this life and be with them in the hour of death,
that all may be gathered into the fold of your eternal kingdom
by the Good Shepherd, our Saviour, Jesus Christ. *Amen.*

Our Father ...   Hail Mary ...

May the peace of our Lord Jesus Christ and the sign of the † holy cross,
the guardianship of angels and the prayers of the just made perfect
   in heaven
defend me from all adversity, visible and invisible. *Amen.*

On going out from home
The Lord preserve my going out and my coming in,
from this time forth for evermore.
O give your angels charge over me,
to keep me in all my ways
and order my steps according to your word. *Amen.*

On embarking on a journey
O God, who led the children of Israel
on dry land through the waters of the Red Sea,
and by a star guided the Magi to the revelation of your glory;
so make my journey safe, and my visit free from anxiety.
Attended by your Angel, bring me to my destination now on earth,
and grant that I may at length attain the haven of eternal salvation;
through Jesus Christ our Lord. *Amen.*

◆ 2 AT DIFFERENT MOMENTS OF THE DAY

Grace before meals
Bless us, O Lord, and these your gifts, of which through your
bounty we are partakers; through Jesus Christ our Lord. *Amen.*

Grace after meals
We give you thanks, almighty God, for these, with all your gifts
and mercies, who lives and reigns for ever and ever. *Amen.*

Other Graces
Lord Jesus be our holy guest,
Our morning prayer,
Our evening rest,
And with this daily food impart
Thy love and grace to every heart. *Amen.*   (Dwight Eisenhower)

Praise God from whom all blessings flow,
Praise him, all creatures here below,
Praise him above, angelic host,
Praise Father, Son, and Holy Ghost. *Amen.*   (Thomas Ken)

Be present at our table, Lord,
Be here and everywhere adored;
These creatures bless, and grant that we
May feast in paradise with thee. *Amen.*   (John Cennick)

Simple prayers in times of need

At the start of any work
O Lord;
prosper the work
of our hands, to the glory
of your name. *Amen.*

In the midst of any work
Let all things be begun,
continued and ended
in your name, and enjoyed
in thankfulness,
O Lord, to your praise
and glory. *Amen.*

Before a conversation
Set a watch, Lord,
upon my tongue,
that I may never
speak a cruel word
which is not true;
or being true,
is not the whole truth;
or being wholly true,
is merciless;
for the love of Jesus Christ.
Amen .

(Michael Buckley)

In temptation
Lord
help me
with your grace,
it is sufficient for me;
in the fire
of my temptations
walk with me
and bid the tempter
to depart. *Amen.*

To assert the presence of God
Where can I go then
from your Spirit?
If I take
the wings of the morning
and dwell
in the uttermost parts of the sea,
even there
your hand shall lead me,
your right hand shall hold me fast.

(Psalm 139)

Daily Devotions

After committing sin
Have mercy on me,
O God,
against you have I sinned
and done evil
in your sight.
Be merciful to me,
a sinner,
for the sake of your Son,
Jesus Christ,
lay not this sin
to my charge,
but create a new
and contrite heart
in me, O Lord. *Amen.*

In sorrow
Why are you
so full of heaviness, O my soul?
and why are you
so disquieted within me?
O put your trust in God;
for I will yet
give him thanks,
who is the help
of my countenance,
and my God. (Psalm 42)

For patience in trials
O Lord,
let me rest in your strength,
understand
through your wisdom,
and embrace your obedience
in the passion
of the cross. *Amen.*

After doing any good thing
Not to me,
O Lord,
not to me,
but to your name
be the praise. *Amen.*

Thanksgiving
Praise the Lord,
O my soul,
and all that is within me
praise his holy name. (Psalm 103)

I will thank you,
Lord,
for you have heard me,
and have become
my salvation. (Psalm 118)

◆ DEVOTIONS TO FOSTER PRAYER

Seeking the Presence of God

Come, Holy Spirit, fill the hearts of your faithful people.
  And kindle in them the fire of your love.
Send forth your Spirit, and they shall be made;
  And you will renew the face of the earth.

O God, who taught the hearts of your faithful people
by the sending to them the light of your Holy Spirit:
grant us by the same Spirit
to have a right judgement in all things
and evermore to rejoice in his holy comfort,
through the merits of Christ Jesus our Saviour. *Amen.*   (*Traditional*)

O God, to whom all hearts are open, all desires known, and from
whom no secrets are hidden; Cleanse the thoughts of our hearts by
the inspiration of your Holy Spirit, that we may perfectly love you,
and worthily magnify your holy Name;
through Christ our Lord. *Amen.*   (*Common Worship*)

O gracious and holy Father, give us wisdom to perceive you,
diligence to seek you, patience to wait for you, eyes to behold you,
a heart to meditate upon you, and a life to proclaim you;
through the power of the Spirit of Jesus Christ our Lord. *Amen.*

(St Benedict)

Father, pour out your Spirit upon your people,
and grant us a new vision of your glory,
a new experience of your power,
a new faithfulness to your Word,
and a new consecration to your service,
that your love may grow among us,
and your kingdom come;
through Christ our Lord. *Amen.*   (The Missions)

Almighty God, who hast given us grace at this time with one accord to make our common supplications unto thee; and dost promise that when two or three are gathered together in thy Name thou wilt grant their requests; fulfil now, O Lord, the desires and petitions of thy servants, as may be most expedient for them; granting us in this world knowledge of thy truth, and in the world to come life everlasting. *Amen.* (St John Chrysostom)

Thanks be to you, my Lord Jesus Christ, for all the benefits you have won for me, for all the pains and insults you have borne for me. Most merciful redeemer, friend and brother, may I know you more clearly, love you more dearly, and follow you more nearly, day by day. *Amen.*

(St Richard of Chichester)

O Lord my God,
teach me to seek you,
for I cannot seek you unless you teach me,
or find you unless you show yourself to me.
Let me seek you in my desire,
let me desire you in my seeking.
Let me find you by loving you,
let me love you when I find you. *Amen.* (St Anselm)

Commemoration of the Holy Trinity

Blessed be the holy and undivided Trinity, one Deity,
    praised and worshipped for ever.
Blessed be the Father in omnipotence,   *praised...*
Blessed be the Son in wisdom,   *praised...*
Blessed be the Holy Spirit in goodness,   *praised...*
Blessed be God in his gifts, and holy in all works,   *praised...*
Blessed be God in heaven and earth, by angels and archangels
  by men and women, by all saints and chosen ones in paradise,   *praised...*
Blessed be God in the most holy sacrament of the altar
  in all the churches and tabernacles of the world. *Amen.*

(from Dies Sacerdotalis)

Before the glorious throne of thy majesty, O Lord,
and the awful judgement-seat of thy burning love,
we thy people do kneel with cherubim and seraphim and archangels,
worshipping, confessing, and praising thee, Lord of all,
Father, Son, and Holy Spirit for ever.   (Syrian Liturgy)

O Trinity most high, most merciful, most bountiful,
Father, Son, and Holy Spirit, one only Deity,
in you I hope: instruct, direct, sustain me.
You are my unique and unchangeable good,
You alone do I seek, do I desire and search for:
Lord, draw me to yourself.
I knock, O Lord; open to me, forsaken and in need.
Plunge me into the depths of your Divinity.
United with you, make me one sole spirit
so that I may possess your infinite riches. *Amen.*   (St Albert the Great)

For the Church

O God of unchangeable power and eternal light,
look favourably on your whole Church, that wonderful and sacred mystery;
and by the tranquil operation of your perpetual providence,
carry out the work of our salvation; that things which were cast down
may be raised up, and that all things may return to unity
through him by whom all things were made,
even your Son, Jesus Christ our Lord. *Amen.*   (*St Gelasius*)

Most gracious Father, we humbly beseech thee
for thy Holy Catholic Church.
Fill it with all truth; in all truth with all peace.
Where it is corrupt, purge it; where it is in error, direct it;
where anything is amiss, reform it; where it is right,
strengthen and confirm it; where it is in want, furnish it;
where it is divided and rent asunder,
make up the breaches of it, O Thou Holy One of Israel. *Amen.*

(*William Laud*)

O God, the Father of our Lord Jesus Christ, our only Saviour, the Prince of Peace:
Give us grace seriously to lay to heart the great dangers we are in by our
unhappy divisions. Take away all hatred and prejudice, and whatsoever else
may hinder us from godly union and concord; that, as there is but one Body,
and one Spirit, and one hope of our calling, one Lord, one faith, one baptism,
one God and Father of us all, so we may henceforth be all of one heart
and of one soul, united in one holy bond of truth and peace, of faith and
charity, and may with one mind and one mouth glorify thee; through
Jesus Christ our Lord.

(*The Book of Common Prayer*)

Acts of Faith, Hope, and Love

of Faith
I believe in you, O Lord,
Almighty, infinitely Wise, and supremely Good;
True and Faithful to your promises, yes, even Truth itself.

You have made me in your own image.
You have redeemed me with your precious blood.
You sanctify me with your ever-renewing Presence.

Lord, I believe: help my unbelief. *Amen.*

of Hope
Out of infinite love, you, O Lord,
have made me an heir of your kingdom
and a joint-heir with Christ.

O good Jesu, to whom else shall I go?
You have the words of eternal life
I hope and I believe in you.

Lord, keep me from despair. *Amen.*

of Love

O eternal Father,
give me the love with which you love the world.
Turn my heart to love of neighbour, as of you.

O triune God, having loved you on earth,
grant that I may love and enjoy you for ever in heaven,
my life, my hope, my joy.

Lord I love, but would love more. *Amen.*

An ascription of praise from the whole creation

You are worthy, O Lord, to receive power
and riches and wisdom and strength
and honour and glory and blessing:
> R/ *We praise and bless your glorious name!*

For your good servants in every age
striving selflessly, faithful to the end. R/

For the wisdom of doctors of the faith,
the zeal of evangelists of the word,
the eloquence of your holy prophets. R/

For the praise of babes, the ministry of women,
the fervour of the young, the experience of the aged
for all the signs of your presence, for all the marks of the cross. R/

For the light of the everlasting gospel
sent to every nation, and kindred, and tongue, and people,
brought to this land by Christian witnesses and missionaries. R/

For the Church, the witness and sign of truth revealed,
the sacramental mystery of Christ in our midst,
for the promise that the gates of hell shall not prevail against it. R/

And so to him who by the power at work within us is able to accomplish
abundantly far more than we can ask or imagine, to him be glory in the Church
and in Christ Jesus to all generations, for ever and ever. *Amen.*

◆ 4 PRAYERS AT NIGHT

Commendation of the day

Examination of conscience:
- How have I spent this past day?
- What gifts of God have I misused?
- What love for God have I not shown?
- Whom have I hurt or offended?
- Have I neglected those who love me?
- Of what things am I ashamed?
- Have I disguised my sins?
- What words do I now wish unspoken?
- What actions do I now wish undone?
- What reparation can I make?
- Did I love my 'neighbour'?
- Did I endeavour to love myself?
- For whom am I duty bound to pray this night?
- For what do I give thanks at the close of this day?

Prayer for Pardon
O God of infinite mercy. Pardon my offences of this day
and cast them into the abyss of your love.
By the death of your dear Son,
forgive the thoughts, words, deeds and omissions
by which I have offended; that by your mercy
I may not die but live and rise to praise you,
O gracious, just, and loving Father. *Amen.*

For those in need

Watch, dear Lord, with those who wake or watch or weep tonight,
and give your angels charge over those who sleep.
Tend your sick ones, O Lord Jesus Christ, rest your weary ones,
bless your dying ones, soothe your suffering ones,
shield your joyous ones, and all for your love's sake. *Amen.*

(St Augustine)

To the Guardian Angel

Angelic spirit, to whose care I am entrusted by God,
guard me ceaselessly and protect me,
visit me and defend me from every assault of the devil.
Cherish me waking and sleeping, night and day,
in every hour and moment: so go with me everywhere
and leave me not, till you have led me to the vision of
my Creator, where, by your aid, I may rejoice with all
the saints. Through the might of Jesus Christ our Lord. *Amen*

(St Anselm)

Commendations

O Lord,
support us all the day long of this troublous life,
until the shades lengthen and the evening comes,
the busy world is hushed, the fever of life is over,
and our work is done. Then, Lord, in your mercy,
grant us safe lodging, a holy rest, and peace
at the last. Through Christ our Lord. *Amen.*

(John Henry Newman)

Look down, O Lord, from thy heavenly throne;
illuminate the darkness of this night with thy celestial brightness;
and from the children of light banish the deeds of darkness;
through Christ our Lord. *Amen*   (St Leo the Great)

Be present, O merciful God, and protect us through the
silent hours of this night, so that we who are fatigued
by the changes and chances of this fleeting world,
may repose upon thy eternal changelessness;
through Jesus Christ our Lord. *Amen*   (St Gelasius)

The general Thanksgiving
Almighty God,
Father of all mercies, we thine unworthy servants
do give thee most humble and hearty thanks
for all thy goodness and loving kindness to us,
and to all men. We bless thee for our creation,
preservation, and all the blessings of this life;
but above all for thine inestimable love
in the redemption of the world by our Lord Jesus Christ;
for the means of grace, and for the hope of glory.
And, we beseech thee, give us that due sense
of all thy mercies, that our hearts may be
unfeignedly thankful, and that we show forth
thy praise, not only with our lips, but in our lives;
by giving up ourselves to thy service, and by
walking before thee in holiness and righteousness
all our days; through Jesus Christ our Lord,
to whom with thee and the Holy Ghost be all
honour and glory, world without end. *Amen*.   (Edward Reynolds)

Benedictions
+ God the Father bless me;
Jesus Christ defend and keep me;
the power of the Holy Spirit enlighten
and sanctify me, this night and for ever. *Amen.*

The Peace of our Lord Jesus Christ,
the purity of the most blessed Virgin Mary,
the sign of the holy + Cross, the might of the
Lord's Passion, the guardianship of the holy Angels,
and the intercession of all the saints,
stand between me and all my foes visible and invisible,
to keep me from all sin, and from every peril to soul
and body, this night and at the hour of my death. *Amen.*

THOU DIDST NOT LEAVE HIS SOUL IN HELL

I ASCEND UNTO MY FATHER AND YOUR FATHER
AND TO MY GOD AND YOUR GOD

NEITHER DIDST THOU SUFFER THINE
HOLY ONE TO SEE CORRUPTION

❺ An Order for Compline

The Lord grant us a quite night, and a perfect end. Amen.

Brethren, be sober, be vigilant; because your adversary the devil, as a
    roaring lion,
walketh about, seeking whom he may devour: whom resist, steadfast in
    the faith. (1 Peter 5:8-9)

But thou, O Lord, have mercy upon us;
       Thanks be to God.

Our help is in the name of the Lord.
       Who hath made heaven and earth.

I confess to Almighty God, to blessed Mary ever-virgin, to blessed Michael
the Archangel, to blessed John the Baptist, to the holy Apostles Peter and
Paul, and to all the Saints, that I have sinned exceedingly in thought, word
and deed, through my fault, through my fault, through my own most
grievous fault. Wherefore I beg blessed Mary ever-virgin, blessed Michael
the Archangel, blessed John the Baptist, the holy Apostles Peter and Paul,
and all the Saints, to pray to the Lord our God for me.

Almighty God have mercy upon us, forgive us all our sins, and bring us to
everlasting life. *Amen.*

✠ Turn us then, O God our Saviour;
       And let thine anger cease from us.

O God, make speed to save me;
       O Lord, make haste to help me.

Glory be … Alleluia. (except in Lent)

Daily Devotions

Psalm 4 *Cum invocarem*

Hear me when I call, O God of my righteousness* thou hast set me at liberty when I was in trouble, have mercy upon me, and harken unto my prayer.

2   O ye sons of men, how long will ye blaspheme mine honour* and have such pleasure in vanity, and seek after leasing?

3   Know this also, that the Lord hath chosen to himself the man that is godly* when I call upon the Lord, he will hear me.

4   Stand in awe and sin not* commune with your own heart, and in your chamber, and be still.

5   Offer the sacrifice of righteousness* and put your trust in the Lord.

6   There be many that say* Who will show us any good?

7   Lord, lift thou up* the light of thy countenance upon us.

8   Thou hast put gladness in my heart* since the time that their corn and wine and oil increased.

9   I will lay me down in peace, and take my rest* for it is thou, Lord, only that makest me dwell in safety.

Glory be …

Psalm 91 *Qui habitat*

Whoso dwelleth under the defence of the most High* shall abide under the shadow of the Almighty.

2   I will say unto the Lord, Thou art my hope, and my stronghold* my God in him will I trust.

3 For he shall deliver thee from the snare of the hunter* and from the noisome pestilence.

4 He shall defend thee under his wings, and thou shalt be safe under his feathers* his faithfulness and truth shall be thy shield and buckler.

5 Thou shalt not be afraid for any terror by night* nor for the arrow that flieth by day.

6 For the pestilence that walketh in darkness* nor for the sickness that destroyeth in the noonday.

7 A thousand shall fall beside thee, and ten thousand at thy right hand* but it shall not come nigh thee.

8 Yea, with thine eyes shalt thou behold* and see the reward of the ungodly.

9 For thou Lord art my hope* thou hast set thine house of defence very high.

10 There shall no evil happen unto thee* neither shall any plague come nigh thy dwelling.

11 For he shall give his Angels charge over thee* to keep thee in all thy ways.

12 They shall bear thee in their hands* that thou hurt not thy foot against a stone.

13 Thou shalt go upon the lion and adder* the young lion and the dragon shalt thou tread under thy feet.

14 Because he hath set his love upon me, therefore will I deliver him* I will set him up because he hath known my Name.

15 He shall call upon me, and I will deliver him* yea, I am with him in trouble; I will deliver him, and bring him to honour.

16 With long life will I satisfy him* and show him my salvation.

Glory be …

Psalm 134 *Ecce nunc*
Behold now praise the Lord: all ye servants of the Lord.

2 Ye that by night stand in the house of the Lord* even in the courts of the house of our God.

3 Lift up your hands in the sanctuary* and praise the Lord.

4 The Lord that made heaven and earth* give thee blessing out of Sion. Glory be ...

Thou, O Lord, art in the midst of us, and we are called by thy Name* leave us not, O Lord, our God.
Thanks be to God   (*Jeremiah* 14:9)

To thee before the close of day,
Creator of the world, we pray,
That with thy wonted favour thou
Wouldst be our guard and keeper now.

From all ill dreams defend our eyes,
From nightly fears and fantasies;
Tread under foot our ghostly foe,
That no pollution we may know.

O Father, that we ask be done,
Through Jesus Christ, thy only Son,
Who, with the Holy Ghost and thee,
Doth live and reign eternally. *Amen.*

Keep me as the apple of an eye;
           Hide me under the shadow of thy wings.

Preserve us, O Lord, while waking, and guard us while sleeping, that awake we may watch with Christ, and asleep we may rest in peace.

> ☩ Lord, now lettest thou thy servant depart in peace: according to thy word.
> For mine eyes have seen: thy salvation,
> Which thou hast prepared: before the face of all people;
> To be a light to lighten the Gentiles: and to be the glory of thy people Israel.
> Glory be...

Preserve us, O Lord, while waking, and guard us while sleeping, that awake we may watch with Christ, and asleep we may rest in peace.

☩ Lord, have mercy upon us.
> Christ, have mercy upon us.
Lord, have mercy upon us.

Our Father ...

O Lord, hear my prayer;
> And let my cry come unto thee.

Visit, we beseech thee, O Lord, this place, and drive from it all the snares of the enemy; let thy holy angels dwell herein to preserve us in peace; and may thy blessing be upon us evermore; through Jesus Christ our Lord. *Amen.*

Let us bless the Lord.
> Thanks be to God.

The almighty and merciful Lord, the Father, the Son, and the Holy Spirit, ☩ bless and preserve us. *Amen.*

Daily Devotions

Anthems to Our Lady

Alma Redemptoris   (From *Advent Sunday to Candlemas*)

Mother of Christ! hear thou thy people's cry,
Star of the deep and portal of the sky!
Mother of him, who thee from nothing made,
Sinking we strive, and call to thee for aid:
O by that joy which Gabriel brought to thee,
Thou Virgin first and last, let us thy mercy see.

Ave Regina Caelorum   (From *Candlemas to Holy Week*)

Hail, O Queen of Heaven enthroned:
Hail, by angels mistress owned:
Root of Jesse, Gate of morn,
Whence the world's true light was born!
Glorious Virgin, joy to thee,
Loveliest whom in heaven they see,
Fairest thou where all are fair,
Plead with Christ our souls to spare.

Regina Coeli   (In *Eastertide*)

Joy to thee, O Queen of heaven, alleluia!
He whom thou wast meet to bear, allelua!
As he promised hath arisen, alleluia!
Pour for us to God thy prayer, alleluia!

Salve Regina   (From *Pentecost to Advent*)

Hail, holy Queen, Mother of Mercy; hail, our life, our sweetness and our
hope! To thee do we cry, poor banished children of Eve; to thee do we
send up our sighs, mourning and weeping in this vale of tears. Turn
then, most gracious advocate, thine eyes of mercy towards us; and after
this our exile, show unto us the fruit of thy womb, Jesus. O clement,
O loving, O sweet Virgin Mary.

◆ 6 PRAYERS IN THE NIGHT

Going to bed
✝ In the Name of the Lord Jesus Christ crucified, I lay down to rest.
Amen.

When lying awake
May thine Angel-guards defend us,
Slumber sweet thy mercy send us,
Holy dreams and hopes attend us,
This livelong night.

Hide me under the shadow of thy wings;
let thy mercy and truth preserve me always.

When lying awake in pain
Lord, by your Cross and Passion,
strengthen me.

Into your hands, O Lord, I commend my spirit;
save me, God of all things.

Hearing a clock strike
My time is in your hand, O Lord.

As the sun rises
Blesssed be the Lord, the God of Israel,
He has visited his people and redeemed them.

O gladsome light, O grace
Of God the Father's face,
The eternal splendour wearing;
Celestial, holy, blest,
Our Saviour Jesus Christ,
Joyful in thine appearing.

Rejoice, O earth, in shining splendour,
Radiant in the brightness of your King!
Christ has conquered! Glory fills you!
Darkness vanishes forever!

O Lord,
as the new day dawns,
may your light rise in our hearts;
come to visit us in the scriptures
and in the breaking of bread
and make us yours for ever.
Through Jesus Christ the Lord. *Amen.*

Devotions for the Holy Eucharist

Participation in the Eucharist focuses for us the individual and communal nature of devotion. We may be silent or alone but we do not pray in private. Prayer is the activity of the Holy Spirit that unites us with Christ, in Christ with all who are his, and through Christ with the Father.

The nature of our individual but corporate communion is summed up by Thomas Aquinas:

> Thousands are, as one, receivers,
> One, as thousands of believers,
> Takes the Food that cannot waste.

Like other devotional forms – icons, statues, candles, incense – the prayers of preparation and thanksgiving offered here can be a way of engaging our senses and managing distractions through the absorbing of our self-awareness. The aim is not isolation from others in worship, but liberation from the confines of self, and abandonment to the inspiration of the Holy Spirit for the fullness of divine worship.

The emphasis of this collection of devotions is therefore extra-liturgical in fostering a right disposition for the celebration of the Eucharist, and the shaping of a joyful, thankful heart with which to go into the world to love and serve the Lord. For this reason this book does not contain an Order of the Eucharist, but is intended to complement whatever rite is customary and the devotional practices it might already provide.

❶ An Order of Preparation

Renewal of baptismal faith

✝ In the name of the Father, and of the Son, and of the Holy Spirit. *Amen.*

An act of repentance and dedication
In baptism God has called me out of darkness into his marvellous light. May he strengthen my faith and renew the grace of my baptism, so that I might die to sin, and rise to live the new life with Christ.

So I resolve afresh this day:

To reject the devil and all rebellion against God.

To renounce the deceit and corruption of evil.

To repent of the sins that separate me from God and neighbour.

And therefore

I turn to Christ as Saviour.

I submit to Christ as Lord.

I come to Christ, the way, the truth and the life.   *(Common Worship – adapted)*

As a statement of baptismal faith you may say the Apostles' Creed (p. 4)

Thanks be to God,
who has received me by baptism into his Church,
and poured upon me the riches of his grace;
may I, in the company of Christ's pilgrim people
be daily renewed by his anointing Spirit,
and come to the inheritance of the saints in glory. *Amen.*

Devotions for days of the week and seasons of the year

SUNDAY – and in Eastertide

Give judgement for me, O God, and defend my cause against an ungodly people;
O deliver me from the deceitful and the wicked.

For you are the God of my refuge; why have you cast me from you?
and why go I so heavily, while the enemy oppresses me?

O send out your light and your truth, that they may lead me,
and bring me to your holy hill and to your dwelling;

That I may go to the altar of God, to the God of my joy and gladness;
and on the lyre I will give thanks to you, O God my God.

Glory ...

(Psalm 43)

Grant me, O Lord, that contrition of heart and flood of tears
through which I might with awe and reverence participate in this banquet,
wherein is present the company of angels and archangels,
earth is joined with heaven, and Christ the risen Lord
is King and Priest and Sacrifice, in the glory of eternity. *Amen.*

Joy with peace, amendment of life,
and the grace and comfort of the Holy Spirit,
grant me, O almighty and merciful Lord. *Amen.*

The Lord is my shepherd; therefore can I lack nothing.

He makes me lie down in green pastures and leads me beside still waters.

He shall refresh my soul and guide me in the paths of righteousness for his name's sake.

Though I walk through the valley of the shadow of death, I will fear no evil; for you are with me; your rod and your staff, they comfort me.

You spread a table before me in the presence of those who trouble me; you anointed my head with oil and my cup shall be full.

Surely, goodness and loving mercy shall follow me all the days of my life; and I will dwell in the house of the Lord for ever.

Glory be …   (Psalm 23)

O Lord,
may the Comforter, proceeding from on high,
illuminate our minds and guide us into all truth,
that we may be rightly prepared to recognise our Lord and Saviour in the
opening of the scriptures and the breaking of bread;
this we ask in Jesu's name. *Amen.*

Joy with peace … (p. 43)

TUESDAY – and at any time of the year

Sing merrily to God our strength shout for joy to the God of Jacob.

Take up the song and sound the timbrel, the tuneful lyre with the harp.

Blow the trumpet at the new moon, as at the full moon, upon our solemn feast-day.

For this is a statute for Israel, a law of the God of Jacob;

The charge he laid on the people of Joseph, when they came out of the land of Egypt.

I am the Lord your God, who brought you out of the land of Egypt, 'Open your mouth wide and I shall fill it.'

Glory be ...   (Psalm 81)

Most gracious God, turn your ear to our prayer,
and enlighten our hearts with the grace of your Holy Spirit,
that we may do you worthy service in these holy mysteries,
and love you with an everlasting love;
through Jesus Christ our Lord. *Amen.*

Joy with peace ... (*p. 43*)

May the Lord hear you in the day of trouble,
the name of the God of Jacob defend you;

Send you help from his sanctuary and strengthen you out of Sion;

Remember all your offerings and accept your burnt sacrifice;

Grant you your heart's desire and fulfil all your mind.

May we rejoice in your salvation and triumph in the name of your God;
may the Lord perform all your petitions.

Now I know that the Lord will save his anointed;
he will answer from his holy heaven, with the mighty strength of his right hand.
Glory be ...   (Psalm 20)

Hear my prayer, O God Most High,
and make me docile to your Holy Spirit.
Form in me a heart with which to love and adore you,
a heart inclined to follow and obey you,
a heart desiring nothing but the satisfaction
of the glory of your presence,
which in this Eucharist you
vouchsafe to us in sacramental form,
through Jesus Christ our Lord. *Amen.*

Joy with peace ... (p. 43)

THURSDAY – and on any Saint's Day

I love the Lord, for he has heard the voice of my supplication;
because he inclined his ear to me on the day I called to him.

I believed that I should perish for I was sorely troubled;
and I said in my alarm, 'Everyone is a liar'

How shall I repay the Lord for all the benefits he has given to me?

I will lift up the cup of salvation and call upon the name of the Lord.

I will fulfil my vows to the Lord in the presence of all his people.

Precious in the sight of the Lord is the death of his faithful servants.

O Lord, I am your servant, the child of your servant;
you have freed me from my bonds.

I will offer to you a sacrifice of thanksgiving and call upon the name of the Lord.
Glory be ...   (Psalm 116)

O good Jesu, true High Priest and pure Victim,
teach me by the Holy Spirit, to approach the altar of your sacrifice
with such reverence, honour, devotion and holy fear,
that (like St N.) I may believe, think, and speak
of the mysteries of your presence in such manner as shall please you,
for my good and that of all who seek and love you. *Amen.*

Joy with peace ... (p. 43)

FRIDAY – and in Lent

The Lord is my light and my salvation; whom then shall I fear?
The Lord is the strength of my life; of whom then shall I be afraid?

When the wicked, even my enemies and my foes, came upon me
to eat up my flesh, they stumbled and fell.

Though a host encamp against me, my heart shall not be afraid;
and though there rise up war against me, yet will I put my trust in him.

For in the day of trouble he shall hide me in his shelter;
and in the secret place of his dwelling shall he hide me
and set me high upon a rock.

And now shall he lift up my head above my enemies round about me;

Therefore will I offer in his dwelling an oblation with great gladness;
I will sing and make music to the Lord.
Glory be ...   (Psalm 27)

Make me a partaker, O Lord my God,
in that abundant feast and banquet of yourself;
may the living Bread come down from heaven
and the fountain of mercy released by
the soldier's lance from your sacred side
refresh, comfort, enlarge and satisfy my soul,
that I may rejoice in your praise and glory for ever. *Amen.*

Joy with peace ... (p. 43)

Bless the Lord, O my soul!
O Lord, how manifold are your works! In wisdom you have made them all;
the earth is full of your creatures.

All of these look to you to give them their food in due season.

When you give it them, they gather it;
you open your hand and they are filled with good.

When you hide your face they are troubled;
when you take away their breath, they die and return again to the dust.

When you send forth your spirit, they are created;
and you renew the face of the earth.

May the glory of the Lord endure for ever;
may the Lord rejoice in his works.
Glory be ...   *(Psalm 104)*

O Lord, almighty God and Father,
as Mary conceived your Son Jesus Christ
by the overshadowing of the Holy Spirit,
so let the invisible and inexpressible Majesty
of that same Spirit descend
upon the bread and wine offered here,
making of our oblations his Body and Blood,
the perfect sacrifice by which our sins are covered,
and we receive the pledge of life eternal,
through Jesus Christ our Lord. *Amen.*

Joy with peace ... (p. 43)

Direction of your intention

O Lord God, Almighty Father,
I make this offering

* for your honour, praise, adoration and glory;

* in remembrance of Christ's death and resurrection;

* in thanksgiving for the blessings bestowed especially on me ...

* for the pardon of all my sins ... and those who sinned against me ...

* for all whom I know to be in need ...

* for those for whom I am duty bound to pray ...

that we who live may complete this pilgrim life in joy,
and they who sleep in Christ may rest in peace and rise in glory. *Amen.*

Take me, O Son of God,
to be a partaker this day of your heavenly banquet;
for I will not tell your secret to your enemies,
I will not betray you with a kiss like Judas,
but, like the thief, confess you:
Remember me, O Lord, in your kingdom. *Amen.*

Prayers before Communion

These are prayers that might be said as a preparation before the celebration of the Eucharist begins, or at the time of communion itself, as you prepare to go to receive the bread of life and the cup of eternal salvation.

Anima Christi
Soul of Christ, sanctify me.
Body of Christ, save me.
Blood of Christ, inebriate me.
Water from the side of Christ, wash me.
Passion of Christ, strengthen me.
Within thy wounds hide me.
Suffer me not to be separated from thee.
From the malicious enemy defend me.
In the hour of my death, call me
And bid me come to thee,
That with thy saints I may praise thee
For ever and ever.

O Sacred Feast!
Wherein Christ is received
His Passion is remembered
Our souls are filled with grace
And the pledge of eternal glory is received.   (Traditional)

Grant, O Lord,
that our bodies may be hallowed by thy holy Body,
and our souls washed in thy propitiatory Blood;
and that they may be for the remission of our sins,
and the pardon of our offences.
O Lord our God, to thee be glory for ever. *Amen.*

(Syrian Liturgy)

Almighty, everlasting God,
behold I approach the sacrament of your Only-begotten Son,
our Lord Jesus Christ.
I come to it as the sick to the physician who will save my life,
unclean I come to the fountain of mercy,
blind, I seek the radiance of eternal light,
poor and needy I draw near to the Lord of heaven and earth;
praying that in your boundless generosity you will deign
to cure my sickness, wash my defilement away, enlighten my blindness,
enrich my poverty, and clothe my nakedness.

   May the Bread of angels, the King of kings and Lord of lords
be received by me with such humble reverence and devout contrition,
such faith and purity, and such good resolutions
as may help the salvation of my soul.

   Grant me grace, I beseech you, to receive
not only the sacrament of our Lord's body and blood
but also its inward power and effect. *Amen.*

(From the Prayer of St Thomas Aquinas)

Spiritual Communion

Receiving Holy Communion is the crown and seal of participation in the Eucharist.

If, for some serious or urgent reason you are unable to receive during the Eucharist, then it is possible to make an act of spiritual communion.

This devotion can also be made when you have been prevented from being present at the Eucharist.

But nothing can substitute for the enrichment of the Church by your presence at its central act of worship, the Eucharist, and the benefit of communion therein received.

An act of Spiritual Communion
Lord Jesus Christ,
saving Victim, Priest divine,
in union with the faithful at every altar of your Church
where your body and blood are offered to the Father,
I make an oblation of praise and thanksgiving.
I believe that you are truly present in the eucharist.
To you I offer my soul, my body and my life.
Come to my heart, embrace me with your love.
Conform my will to the pattern of your perfect obedience,
so that loving all that you love, I may never be separated from you,
but live to the glory of the Father.
Amen.

Our Father ...

The *Anima Christi* (*see above, p. 51*)

Blessed, praised, hallowed and adored
be Jesus Christ on his throne of glory,
and in the most holy Sacrament of the altar.

✝ The grace of our Lord Jesus Christ, and the love of God,
and the fellowship of the Holy Spirit, be with us all, evermore. *Amen.*

This devotion may also be enriched in the following ways:

• Begin with the order of preparation given above (p. 42)
• If possible, find and read the passages of scripture appointed for the day.
• Identify your devotion with some specific intention. (see p. 50)
• Make your act of spiritual communion.
• Offer your devotional thanksgiving.
• Make your financial offering.

Thanksgivings after Communion

Various prayers

Thanks be to you, my Lord Jesus Christ,
for all the benefits you have won for me,
for all the pains and insults you have borne for me.
O most merciful redeemer, friend and brother,
may I know you more clearly,
love you more dearly,
and follow you more nearly,
day by day. *Amen.*   (St Richard of Chichester)

God our Father,
in this most wonderful Sacrament
we come into the presence of Jesus Christ your Son,
born of the Virgin Mary, and crucified for our salvation.
May we who declare our faith in this fountain of love and goodness,
drink from it always the water of eternal life;
through Jesus Christ our Lord. *Amen.*

Holy Michael the Archangel, defend us in the day of battle;
be our safeguard against the wickedness and snares of the devil,
may God rebuke him, we humbly pray.
And by the power of God, trample Satan underfoot
and all wickedness present in the world for the ruin of souls.

(Traditional)

Lord Jesus Christ,
I give you my hands to do your work.
I give you my feet to go your way.
I give you my eyes to see as you see.
I give you my tongue to speak your words.
I give you my mind that you may think in me.
I give you my spirit that you may pray in me.
Above all,
I give you my heart that you may love, in me,
your Father and all mankind.
I give you my whole self that you may grow in me,
so that it is you, Lord Jesus,
who live and work and pray in me. *Amen.*

(attributed to Lancelot Andrews)

The mystery of your dispensation, O Christ our God,
has been accomplished as far as in us lies.
We have seen the memory of your death.
We have seen the sign of your resurrection.
We have been filled with your endless life.
We have enjoyed your heavenly delights,
of which we pray that hereafter
you will make us worthy.
Through the grace of God the Father,
and of the Holy, Good, and
Life-giving Spirit
✝ let me go hence in peace
to love and serve you in the world. *Amen.*

(Liturgy of St Basil)

Blessed, praised, hallowed and adored be Jesus
on his throne of glory;
and in the most holy sacrament of the altar.

Thanksgivings for days of the week and seasons of the year

SUNDAY — and in Eastertide

Bless the Lord all you works of the Lord:
> R/ *Sing his praise and exalt him for ever.*

Bless the Lord you heavens: R/

Bless the Lord you angels of the Lord: R/

O people of God bless the Lord: R/

Bless the Lord you priests of the Lord: R/

Bless the Lord you servants of the Lord: R/

Bless the Lord all you that are holy and humble in heart: R/

Lord Jesus Christ,
set as a seal upon me the marks of your most holy body,
glorified in heaven and truly present in the Eucharist:
sign my feet, that I may follow in your steps;
sign my hands, that I may use them in your service;
sign my side, that I may issue in praise of that majestic glory
in which you reign with the Father and the Holy Spirit
for all eternity. *Amen.*

Let us bless the Lord.
> Thanks be to God.

✝ May the souls of the departed, through the mercy of God, rest in peace. *Amen.*

Blessed are you, the God of our ancestors:
>R/ *Worthy to be praised and exalted for ever.*

Blessed is your holy and glorious name: R/

Blessed are you, in your holy and glorious temple: R/

Blessed are you who look into the depths: R/

Blessed are you, enthroned on the cherubim: R/

Blessed are you on the throne of your kingdom: R/

Blessed are you in the heights of heaven: R/

All glory, thanks and praise to you,
Lord Jesus Christ, shepherd slain and risen king.
I, the sheep that you have sought,
ransomed, and fed with your own self, surrender my life to you.
Make me often mindful of your love, thankful for your presence,
and hopeful in pursuit of you, my joy and consolation,
now and for eternity. *Amen.*

Let us bless the Lord.
>Thanks be to God.

✝ May the souls of the departed, through the mercy of God, rest in peace. *Amen.*

TUESDAY — and on any Saint's Day

How good it is to make music for our God, how joyful to honour him with praise.

The Lord builds up Jerusalem and gathers together the outcasts of Israel.

He heals the brokenhearted and binds up all their wounds.

He counts the number of the stars and calls them all by their names.

Great is our Lord and mighty in power; his wisdom is beyond all telling.

Glory be ...   (Psalm 147)

O sweet Lord Jesus,
transfix the affections of my inmost soul
with the healthful wound of your most joyous love,
with true, serene, holy and apostolic charity;
that following in the footsteps of your saints
I may serve you in gladness,
and discern in all your creatures
the mark of your ineffable beauty. *Amen.*

Let us bless the Lord.
          Thanks be to God.

✝ May the souls of the departed, through the mercy of God, rest in peace. *Amen.*

Devotions for the Holy Eucharist

WEDNESDAY – and in Advent

Sing Praise to the Lord, O Jerusalem; praise your God, O Sion;

For he has strengthened the bars of your gates and has blest your children within you.

He has established peace on your borders and satisfies you with the finest wheat.

He sends forth his command to the earth and his word runs very swiftly.

He gives snow like wool and scatters the hoarfrost like ashes.

He casts down his hailstones like morsels of bread; who can endure his frost?

He sends forth his word and melts them; he blows with his wind and the waters flow.

Glory be ...   (Psalm 147ii)

Almighty and everlasting God,
receive with pity the sacrifice offered to the glory of your name
and for the salvation of all, living and departed.
Deliver your people from every evil,
and when you come in judgement open to us the gates of paradise;
through Jesus Christ our Lord. *Amen.*

Let us bless the Lord.
          Thanks be to God.

+ May the souls of the departed, through the mercy of God, rest in peace. *Amen.*

(Alleluia — except in Lent)
Give praise, you servants of the Lord, O praise the name of the Lord.

Blessed be the name of the Lord, from this time forth and for evermore.

From the rising of the sun to its setting, let the name of the Lord be praised.

The Lord is high above all nations, and his glory above the heavens.

Who is like the Lord our God, that has his throne so high,
yet humbles himself to behold the things of heaven and earth?

Glory be ...   (Psalm 113)

Lord Jesus Christ, to you I return humble thanks
for the inexpressible riches given and received in communion.
Be for ever my hope and confidence,
my peace, enjoyment, fragrance and refreshment;
be my refuge, help, wisdom and treasure
in whom I am immovably fixed, now and forever. *Amen.*

Let us bless the Lord.
        Thanks be to God.

✝ May the souls of the departed, through the mercy of God, rest in peace. *Amen.*

I love the Lord, for he has heard the voice of my supplication;
because he inclined his ear to me on the day I called to him.

The snares of death encompassed me; the pains of hell took hold of me;
by grief and sorrow I was held.

Then I called upon the name of the Lord: 'O Lord, I beg you, deliver my soul.'

Gracious is the Lord and righteous; our God is full of compassion.

The Lord watches over the simple; I was brought very low and he saved me.

Glory be … (Psalm 116)

Lord Jesus Christ, let not death destroy this body,
but by the triumph of your cross rebuild in us the temple of your glory;
dwell in our midst in your sacrament of love,
enthroned upon the praises of our hearts for ever and ever. *Amen.*

Let us bless the Lord.
Thanks be to God.

+ May the souls of the departed, through the mercy of God, rest in peace. *Amen.*

SATURDAY – and at Christmas

(Alleluia – except in Lent)
O sing to the Lord a new song; sing his praise in the congregation of the faithful.

Let Israel rejoice in their maker; let the children of Zion be joyful in
their king.

Let them praise his name in the dance; let them sing praise to him with timbrel
and lyre.

For the Lord has pleasure in his people and adorns the poor with salvation.

Let the faithful be joyful in glory; let them rejoice in their ranks:

Glory be ...   (Psalm 149)

O God, our Father,
unite us who partake of the one bread and one cup
in the communion of the one Holy Spirit;
abiding in your love may we, with all the saints,
join the praises of seraphim and angels:
for in the condescension of your Son you have joined earth to heaven,
ended our exile, and brought us back to our eternal home,
where you dwell in glory, now and for ever. *Amen.*

Let us bless the Lord.
          Thanks be to God.

+ May the souls of the departed, through the mercy of God, rest in peace. *Amen.*

Devotions for the Seasons and the Saints

The passing of time is sanctified by the liturgical seasons in which the mystery of redemption is unfolded. In a similar way the sanctification of the pilgrim people of God is acclaimed in the lives of the saints on their feast days.

Devotion in the seasons and to the saints thus irradiates the raw material of life in time and in persons. It is a celebration of Christian hope and identity. The seasonal devotions offered here may help to add distinctive colour to daily devotions, perhaps in Morning and Evening Prayers, or as part of the preparation and thanksgiving for the Eucharist. A calendar of saints' days is also included in this section, providing an opportunity to claim the communion of saints as a part of our routine, but also as a channel of intercession: for the homeland, distinctive work, or legacy of a particular saint, and for those people, institutions, and churches under his or her patronage.

As with all prayer, these devotions are not intended to be burdensome observations, but joyful intrusions into the everyday routine of yet another shaft of heavenly glory. These are holy-day/holiday opportunities. Enjoy!

Devotions for the Seasons

Advent

The Collect for Advent
Almighty God, give us grace to cast away the works of darkness
and to put on the armour of light, now in the time of this mortal life,
in which your Son Jesus Christ came to us in great humility;
that on the last day, when he shall come again in his glorious majesty
to judge the living and the dead, we may rise to the life immortal;
through him who is alive and reigns with you, in the unity of the Holy Spirit,
one God, now and for ever. *Amen*

The Book of Common Prayer provides for this collect to be said every day in Advent.

A Devotion for the 7 days before Christmas

The Great Antiphons

Each of these antiphons on Christ's fulfilment of the Old Testament are associated with Mary's canticle, the Magnificat, on the seven days leading up to Christmas.

December 17th   O Sapientia
O WISDOM, which came forth from the mouth of the Most High, reaching from one end to the other mightily, and sweetly ordering all things: Come and teach us the way of prudence.

December 18th   O Adonai
O LORD AND RULER of the House of Israel, who appeared to Moses in a flame of fire in the bush, and gave to him the Law in Sinai: Come, and redeem us with an outstretched arm.

December 19th   O Radix Jesse
O ROOT OF JESSE, who stands for an ensign of the people, before whom kings are silent, and to whom the nations pray: Come, and deliver us, and do not delay.

December 20th   O Clavis David
O KEY OF DAVID, and sceptre of the House of Israel, who opens and no one closes, and closes and no one opens: Come, and loose the prisoner from the prison-house, and those that sit in darkness and the shadow of death.

December 21st   O Oriens
O DAYSPRING, Brightness of the Eternal Light, and Sun of Righteousness: Come, and enlighten those who sit in darkness and the shadow of death.

December 22nd   O Rex Gentium
O KING OF THE NATIONS, their Desire and Corner-stone, who makes both one: Come, and save the human race whom you formed from the dust of the earth.

December 23rd   O Emmanuel
O EMMANUEL, our King and Lawgiver, the Desire of all nations, and their Saviour: Come, and save us, O Lord our God.

Devotions for the Seasons and the Saints

On Christmas Eve

O Judah and Jerusalem, do not fear, or be dismayed; tomorrow go forth, for the Lord will be with you.

May God almighty,
who by the incarnation of his only-begotten Son
scattered the darkness of the world
and enlightened this most holy night,
drive far from our lives the darkness of sin,
filling us with the light of his presence.

God sent angels to summon shepherds
to witness the mystery of his incarnation;
may he pour out his grace upon us this night
and in the dawn of the age to come
be our Shepherd in the pastures of everlasting joy.

May he, who through his incarnation
united earthly things with heavenly,
fill us with the bliss of inward peace
and make us partakers with the heavenly host.

For
while all things were in quiet silence, and night was in the midst of her swift course, your Almighty Word, O Lord, leaped down out of your royal throne. Alleluia.

Christmastide

A Christmas Responsory
Today the King of Heaven deigns for our sake to be born of a Virgin, and to recall lost humanity to the heavenly kingdom. Let the army of angels rejoice, for eternal salvation appears to the human race.
Mercy and truth are met together. Alleluia.
Righteousness and peace have kissed each other. Alleluia.
Glory to God in the Highest, and on earth peace to people of good will.

A Christmas Acclamation
It is our duty and our joy
that we should at all times and in all places
lift up our hearts on high;
and give adoration to the
Divine Mystery
which stops the old and earthly law,
marvellously restoring
the substance of our human nature
and bringing it forth fresh and heavenly;
that what God's grace is now effecting
might be celebrated
in the rejoicings of his Church.

Prayers at the Crib.

Blessed be Jesus, true God and true man, born on earth as one like us.
Blessed be Jesus, heaven is your throne, yet you chose a stable for your birth.
Blessed be Jesus, Lord of all creation, yet for us cradled in a manger.
Blessed be Jesus, beloved Son of the eternal Father, yet suckled at the breast of Mary.
Blessed be Jesus, the Guardian of our souls, entrusted now to Joseph's watchful care.
Blessed be Jesus, mighty Word of God's creation, now adored by ox and ass.
Blessed be Jesus, Shepherd of Israel, now shepherds acclaim your heavenly birth.
Blessed be Jesus, Wisdom and Power of God, royal gifts manifest your glory,

For you alone are the Holy One,
you alone are the Lord,
you alone are the Most High, Jesus Christ,
with the Holy Spirit,
in the glory of God the Father. *Amen.*

O Son of the Living God, Jesus Christ,
we worship in spirit before your holy manger
and we adore you, Holy Child and King of Angels.
Of your goodness, remember our weakness;
banish our fears and pardon our sins,
grant us humility and gentleness of heart,
so that we may grow into your likeness
and hereafter be received into your eternal kingdom,
where you live with the Father and the Holy Spirit,
for ever and ever. *Amen.*

O blessed Spirit,
by the nativity of our Lord Jesus Christ
fill the Church and the whole world
with light and joy and peace.
Hasten the day when Christ will come again,
when the elect are gathered in,
the just perfected,
and his kingdom seen on earth in all its justice.
This we ask, through Christ the Lord. *Amen.*

O holy Child of Bethlehem,
be born in us, we pray.

Almighty God,
who hast given us thy only-begotten Son to take our nature upon him,
and as at this time to be born of a pure Virgin; Grant that we being regenerate,
and made thy children by adoption and grace, may daily be renewed by thy
Holy Spirit; through the same our Lord Jesus Christ, who liveth and reigneth
with thee and the same Spirit, ever one God, world without end. *Amen.*

Litany of the Word-Incarnate, our Lord Jesus Christ

Lord, have mercy.

Christ, have mercy.

Lord, have mercy.

O Christ, hear us.

O Christ, graciously hear us.

O God, the Father of heaven, R/ *Have mercy upon us.*

O God, the Son, Redeemer of the world,

O God, the Holy Spirit,

Holy Trinity, one God,

O Word, made flesh,

O Word, full of grace and truth,

O Word of the Lord,

God by whom all things were made,

Lord God of Israel, Blessed for ever,

Emmanuel, God with us,

Beloved Son, in whom the Father is well-pleased,

Whose Name is above every name,

Upholding all things by your power,

The First-born of all creation,

The First-born among many,

Expectation of the nations,

Wonderful, Counsellor, the Mighty God,

Seed of Abraham,

Star risen out of Jacob,

Lion of the tribe of Judah,

Stem of Jesse,

Son of David,

Son of Man,

Jesus of Nazareth,

Child of Mary, At whose name every knee shall bow,

In whom is the fullness of the Godhead,

Christ, our peace, making both One,

Brightness of the Everlasting Light,

Express Image of the Person of God,

Tree of Life, The Beginning and the End,

God blessed for ever,

Lamb of God, you take away the sins of the world, have mercy on us.

Lamb of God, you take away the sins of the world, have mercy on us.

Lamb of God, you take away the sins of the world, grant us peace.

Our Father ...

Most merciful and loving God,
through your will Jesus Christ our Lord
humbled himself that he might exalt creation;
he took flesh
that he might restore your image in us
and was born of the Virgin
that he might uphold the lowly.
Grant us the inheritance of the meek;
perfect in us your likeness
and bring us at last to your beauty,
that we may glorify your grace;
through Jesus Christ our Lord. *Amen.*

Evening antiphon for the Feast of the Epiphany
Three wonders mark this day we celebrate:
Today the star led the Magi to the manger;
Today water was changed into wine at the marriage feast;
Today Christ desired to be baptized by John in the river Jordan
to bring us salvation, alleluia.

(Catholic Prayerbook)

An Epiphany Acclamation
It is our duty and our joy
that we should at all times and in all places
give praise to you, O God,
wonderful in your works
by which the mysteries of your Kingdom
have been revealed.
For there went out before this joyful event
A Star,
sign of a virgin in childbirth,
to declare to the astounded magi
the earthly nativity of the King of Heaven,
that God manifested in the world
might be announced by a heavenly sign;
that brought forth in the fullness of time
he might by the things of time be made known.
To God be glory for ever.

(Roman Breviary)

O God, who by the leading of a star didst manifest thy only-begotten Son to
the Gentiles: Mercifully grant, that we, which know Thee now by faith, may
after this life have the fruition of Thy glorious Godhead; through Jesus Christ
our Lord. *Amen.*

Devotions for the Seasons and the Saints

Lent and Holy Week

For the blessing of our Lenten Discipline

Behold, now is the acceptable time; this is the day of salvation.

Grant us, Lord,
to begin this period of Christian exercise
by holy fasting.
In our encounter with the spirits of evil
help and defend us
with the armour of self-denial.
Through Jesus Christ our Lord. *Amen.*

O Lord,
grant that as our bodies grow weaker
in this season of self-denial,
so our souls may grow stronger.
Strengthen us in our resistance to sin,
encourage us in the desire for righteousness,
that abstaining from the fruits of the earth
we may bear more abundantly the fruits of your Spirit;
through Jesus Christ our Lord. *Amen.*

The Collect for Ash Wednesday
Almighty and everlasting God,
you hate nothing that you have made
and forgive the sins of all those who are penitent:
create and make in us new and contrite hearts
that we, worthily lamenting our sins
and acknowledging our wretchedness
may receive from you, the God of all mercy,
perfect remission and forgiveness;
through Jesus Christ our Lord. *Amen.*

The Book of Common Prayer provides for this collect to be said every day in Lent.

The Stations of the Cross

+ In the name of the Father, and of the Son, and of the Holy Spirit. Amen.

Jesus our Saviour,
the path that I intend to follow
was marked by your sweat and blood;
it saw you despised and rejected.
Give all who walk this road
the spirit of true penitence,
and help me to bear
with courage and patience
all the crosses and humiliations
in the pilgrimage of life,
knowing that I am following you.

At each station you may say:
We adore you, O Christ, and we bless you.
Because by your holy cross you have redeemed the world.

And make an act of contrition:
O God, I love you with my whole heart, and above all things,
and am heartily sorry that I have offended you. May I never
offend you any more. May I love you without ceasing, and
make it my delight to do in all things your most holy will.

And you may add:
Our Father ...
Hail Mary ...
Glory ...

1   Jesus is condemned to death.

Pilate said to him, 'Do you hear how many charges they have brought against you?' But to the governor's amazement, he offered no reply.

Reflection

Pilate sits in judgement: Jesus stands condemned. He stands with all who throughout history suffer persecution, destruction, injustice, calumny, war, the pride of others, and abuse. At this moment, the Word by whom the heavens and the earth were made embraces the silence known to every victim. From the cross there will be one last exultant cry: It is accomplished. The victim slain will rise again as the Lamb triumphant who gives voice in judgement for those who have stood with him.

Jesus, help us not to judge others. Be merciful when you judge us who are sinners. Our Father …

2   Jesus receives his cross.

They then took charge of Jesus, and carrying his own cross he went out of the city to the place of the skull or, as it was called in Hebrew, Golgotha.

Reflection

Blessed are you when people abuse you and persecute you …

Jesus identifies the blessedness of the abused and persecuted with prophecy. Persecution can be the response of the un-free towards those who are no longer bound within restrictions that limit the ability to speak the word of God, particularly when that word is a hard one to hear and accept. Truth in the person of the Word was disconcerting to Pilate and he had it silenced for the sake of a quiet life. Are we not similarly tempted sometimes?

Jesus, help us not to impose burdens on others through fear and selfishness.
Sacred heart of Jesus,
Have mercy on us.

3   Jesus falls for the first time.

Harshly dealt with, he bore it humbly, he never opened his mouth, like a lamb that is led to the slaughter-house, like a sheep that is dumb before its shearers.

Reflection

. . . and speak all kinds of calumny against you.

A fall in public is embarrassing, but people generally come forward to offer help. Not in this case. Jesus is alone. The force and extent of his humiliation are as relentless as the ground that rises up to hit him. Calumny, for all that it is a spoken thing, is no less real in its effect. A single word can destroy trust, dignity, hope, and life itself. Think of the word that betrayed Anne Frank to the Nazis. And once spoken, we cannot take that word back. It is our judgement.

Jesus, give us the strength to protect those who are weak and oppressed.
Lamb of God, you take away the sins of the world, have mercy on us.
Lamb of God, you take away the sins of the world, have mercy on us.
Lamb of God, you take away the sins of the world, grant us peace.

4   Jesus meets his mother.

All you who pass this way, look and see: is there any sorrow like the sorrow that afflicts me? How can I describe you, to what compare you, daughter of Jerusalem?

Reflection

Blessed are the peacemakers.

As Jesus meets his mother the recollection of peace is a refreshment that evokes the safety of home. Peace is not the absence of physical exertion or the elimination of difficult emotions, but a deeper sense of connectedness that mutually enhances dignity, trust and love. Here we might paraphrase: blessed are the homemakers, the people who offer from what they have an environment in which others find a welcome that betokens the generosity of the Holy Spirit, so evident in Mary's life.

Jesus, enfold our homes and families with the joy and peace of your home in Nazareth.

Hail Mary ...

5   Simon of Cyrene helps Jesus to carry his cross.

As they were leading him away they seized on a man, Simon from Cyrene, who was coming in from the country, and made him shoulder the cross and carry it behind Jesus.

(Luke 23:26)

Reflection
Blessed are those persecuted in the cause of right.

The consolation for them is simply stated: 'for theirs is the kingdom of heaven.' The subsequent parables in Jesus' teaching indicate that there are many surprising ways to participate in the life of the kingdom; prostitutes make their way in before Pharisees, for example. The perception that justice is the kernel of righteousness permits the inclusion in the kingdom of many whose heroic living out of its values might call our own priorities into question. Would I risk being a Simon of Cyrene?

Jesus, let us see you in the face of every human being made in the image of God. Glory …

6   Veronica wipes the face of Jesus.

I tell you solemnly, in so far as you did this to one of the least of these brothers of mine, you did it to me.

(Matthew 25:40)

Reflection
Blessed are those who show mercy.

The consolation of this beatitude is a mirror image: 'mercy will be shown them.' For Veronica, as has fascinated religious artists throughout the centuries, the consolation is the imprint of the face of Jesus. In our photographic age the notion of a 'true likeness' (the meaning of the name, Veronica) has become a technical matter of little merit or significance. But for the person seeking blessedness it is a moral, spiritual matter in which there can be discerned a deeper resemblance – the image of God.

Jesus, let us seek pardon where there is injury, let us bring hope where there is despair.
Kyrie eleison, Christe eleison, Kyrie eleison.

7   Jesus falls the second time.

I made no resistance, neither did I turn away. I offered my back to those who struck me, my cheeks to those who tore at my beard; I did not cover my face against insult or spittle.   (Isaiah 50:5-6)

Reflection

Blessed are those who hear the word of God and keep it.

In Christian devotion the cross is viewed as a tool or instrument: of death, but more significantly in the creation of new life. The image of the cultivation of the earth suggests itself, with the cross as a plough with which Jesus has first cleared the debris of our neglected and overgrown lives, making us ready to keep, or plant, the seed of the gospel. When the cross presses heavily upon you, the footprint of the master gardener is close by, preparing you with skill and loving care for tender new growth.

Jesus, give us the courage to face what is painful and unattractive; may your love cast out our fear.
Our Father ...

8   Jesus speaks to the women of Jerusalem.

Large numbers of people followed him, and of women too, who mourned and lamented for him. But Jesus turned to them and said, 'Daughters of Jerusalem, do not weep for me; weep rather for yourselves and for your children.' (Luke 23:27-28)

Reflection

Weep for yourselves and for your children.

The capacity to weep is one that we regard with suspicion. Tears can be produced in synthetic emotion, and we probably know when we are indulging in that or being willingly manipulated by media use of this power. The danger with such misuse of our tears is that we might damage an important capacity and gift: the physical manifestation of deep compassion, an expression and symbol that is more eloquent than words. True tears are a gift to lavish on others and ourselves with great care.

Jesus, prevent us from being superficial; help us to identify the things that really matter.
Lord, by your cross and resurrection you have set us free; you are the saviour of the world.

9   Jesus falls for the third time.

Here are we preaching a crucified Christ; to the Jews an obstacle that they cannot get over, to the pagans madness, but to those who have been called, whether they are Jews or Greeks, a Christ who is the power and the wisdom of God. For God's foolishness is wiser than human wisdom, and God's weakness is stronger than human strength.

(1 Corinthians 1:23-25)

Reflection
Blessed are the poor in spirit.

The description 'poor in spirit' is not an excuse for disregarding material poverty. But the identification of poverty in spirit points us to those who are so easily overlooked or whom we impoverish by a thoughtless word or gesture. What we describe as self-esteem is that measure by which worth is recognized. Only when we perceive the reality of this worth in the sight of God do we learn the importance of raising the fallen, embracing the lost, and giving thanks for our own rescue in Christ.

Jesus, deepen our faith in the Father's love. Help us to understand that the everlasting arms will never allow us to fall.
Glory …

10   Jesus is stripped of his garments.

When the soldiers had finished crucifying Jesus they took his clothing and divided it into four shares, one for each soldier. His undergarment was seamless, woven in one piece from neck to hem; so they said to one another, 'Instead of tearing it, let's throw dice to decide who is to have it.'

(John 19:23)

Reflection
Blessed are the lowly.

We see the process of stripping differently according to need and context. With a picture or piece of furniture in need of repair, it is an essential part of the process of restoration. With a person, as a public spectacle, it seems to be a sign of degradation. But perhaps blessedness comes at the cost of being stripped; for us, too, it's part of the process of restoration. The recovery of 'true lowliness of heart' lies in the stripping away of pride, fear, and the defensiveness that makes us other than we really are.

Jesus, teach us to value in this life the things which last to eternity.
Sacred heart of Jesus, have mercy on us.

11 Jesus is nailed to the cross.

They crucified him there and the two criminals also, one on the right, the other on the left. Jesus said, 'Father, forgive them; they do not know what they are doing.' One of the criminals spoke up, 'Jesus,' he said, 'remember me when you come into your kingdom.' 'Indeed, I promise you,' he replied, 'today you will be with me in paradise.'   (Luke 23:33-34)

Reflection
Blessed are the pure in heart.

In group discussion about the beatitudes, this one about the pure in heart often emerges as the favourite. Why? Perhaps because vision is the sense by which our curiosity is most immediately satisfied. To want to see God is the obvious expression of our longing to know God. But if the promise to the repentant thief is our guide, purity of heart as the condition for the vision of God depends first on seeing ourselves as we really are. Only a contrite, loving heart can sustain the intensity of paradise.

Jesus, take from us all bitterness and envy of others; let us give thanks for all we have received from you.
Lamb of God ...

12 Jesus dies on the cross.

From the sixth hour there was darkness all over the land until the ninth hour. And at about the ninth hour, Jesus cried out in a loud voice, 'My God, my God, why have you deserted me?' ... Then Jesus cried again with a loud voice and breathed his last. At that moment the curtain of the temple was torn in two, from top to bottom.   (Matthew 27:45-46,50-51)

Reflection
Blessed are those who hunger and thirst for what is right.

Hunger and thirst are very physical sensations that point to a need for material satisfaction. So 'what is right' also pertains to this sphere, as the ordering of creation in the way God intended. Blessedness is exposed on the cross in Jesus' act of re-ordering a disoriented world. The action is material, as it is spiritual and eternal, and within it emerges the source of our satisfaction. The torn curtain gives access to the holy of holies – eternity, while blood and water satisfy us now in sacramental signs.

Soul of Christ ... (p. 51)

13   Jesus is taken down from the cross.

After this, Joseph of Arimathaea, who was a disciple of Jesus, though a secret one because he was afraid of the Jews, asked Pilate to let him remove the body of Jesus. Pilate gave permission. (John 19:38,41-42)

Reflection
Blessed are you who are poor.

Being and having are linked. We can dismantle people's dignity by the way in which we take their possessions. Even the redistribution of misappropriated or improper wealth must be characterized by transparency and justice, or new injustices will surely follow. But when the body of Jesus is taken down from the cross, the justice of God's mercy begins to be revealed, as properties are redistributed. What we had and he had not is now his: our death, taken lovingly, and from which we derive new life.

Jesus, even in adversity give us joy, for joy is the mark of our confidence in the Father's love.
Hail Mary ...

14   Jesus is laid in the sepulchre.

Joseph took the body, wrapped it in a clean shroud and put it in his own new tomb which he had hewn out of the rock. He then rolled a large stone across the entrance of the tomb and went away. (Matthew 27:59-60)

Reflection
Blessed are those who mourn.

Grief is human, as death is. The reality of the incarnation is thus profoundly expressed at the tomb of Lazarus: 'Jesus wept.' Though it can turn us in on ourselves, grief is not essentially selfish; it is the expression of love for another, and the registering that, capable of loving and being loved, we experience a new, painful limitation when the receiver and giver of our love dies. Blessedness is found in having loved; consolation in living the eternally reciprocated love of the Trinity.

Jesus, teach us to know you, to love you, to follow you; call us on the last day to share in your resurrection.
Glory ...

For us Christ became obedient, even to accepting death on the cross.

Lord Jesus Christ,
let your passion be my strength
whereby I am fenced, protected, and defended.
Let your wounds be my nurture
whereby I am fed, inebriated, and refreshed.
Let the sprinkling of your blood
be the cleansing of my sins.
Let your death
be my gateway to eternal glory.
In these let me find health,
longing, desire and joy
in body and in soul,
now and for ever. *Amen*   (St Gregory)

Be mindful, Lord, of this your family,
for whose sake our Lord Jesus Christ, was betrayed,
yielded himself into his enemies' hands,
and undertook the agony of the cross:
who now lives and reigns with you and the Holy Spirit,
God, for ever and ever. *Amen*.

May the divine assistance remain with us always.
✠ May the souls of the faithful departed, through the mercy of God, rest in peace.
Amen.

Before the Crucifix
Lord, by this sweet and saving Sign,
defend us from our foes and thine.

Jesu, by thy wounded feet, Direct our path aright:
Jesu, by thy nailed hands, Move ours to deeds of love:
Jesu, by thy pierced side, Cleanse our desires:
Jesu, by thy crown of thorns, Annihilate our pride;
Jesu, by thy silence, Shame our complaints:
Jesu, by thy parched lips, Curb our cruel speech:
Jesu, by thy closing eyes, Look on our sin no more:
Jesu, by thy broken heart, Knit ours to thee.

And by this sweet and saving Sign,
Lord, draw us to our peace and thine.   (Richard Crawshaw – adapted)

A Litany based on St Bridget's Prayers on the Passion

O Jesus! Maker of the world, holding the earth in the hollow of your hand,
call to mind the nailing of your hands to the wood of the cross of our salvation:
And remember me in the glory of your kingdom.

O Jesus! Heavenly physician, bruised in rendered limbs upon the cross,
call to mind your prayer for the forgiveness of your enemies:
And remember me in the glory of your kingdom.

O Jesus! The very Glory of Angels, and Paradise of delights,
call to mind the blows, the spittle, and the tearing of flesh in your Passion:
And remember me in the glory of your kingdom.

O Jesus! Mirror of everlasting love,
call to mind our wretchedness mirrored in your disfigured Majesty:
And remember me in the glory of your kingdom.

O Jesus! King most lovely, and dearest Lover of humanity,
call to mind the sword that pierced your only comforter, the Mother of our Hope:
And remember me in the glory of your kingdom.

O Jesus! Unfailing Spring of love,
call to mind that depth from which you said, "I thirst":
And remember me in the glory of your kingdom.

O Jesus! Very Sweetness to the heart and soul,
call to mind the bitter gall and vinegar of our sins:
And remember me in the glory of your kingdom.

O Jesus! Royal in might and of thrilling presence,
call to mind the dereliction of abandonment at the moment of your death:
And remember me in the glory of your kingdom.

O Jesus! Alpha and Omega, everlasting Life and Strength,
call to mind the length and breadth of your suffering on the cross:
And remember me in the glory of your kingdom.

O Jesus! Unfathomed Depth of loving pity,
call to mind the piercing sorrow of your wounded heart:
And remember me in the glory of your kingdom.

O Jesus! Mirror of truth, Sign of unity, Bond of charity,
call to mind the scourging of your flesh, assumed in the Virgin's womb:
And remember me in the glory of your kingdom.

O Jesus! Lion of the tribe of Judah, King eternal and invincible,
call to mind that grief when strength gave way and you said, "It is finished":
And remember me in the glory of your kingdom.

O Jesus! Only-begotten of the Father, Brightness and Image of his Substance,
call to mind the yearning effort with which you gave yourself into his hands:
And remember me in the glory of your kingdom.

O Jesus! True and fruitful vine,
call to mind the blood you shed when you trod the wine-press of the cross alone:
And remember me in the glory of your kingdom.

By this bitter passion,
by this remembrance of your mercy
by this sorrow,
grant the remission of my sins
and the gift of life eternal.

Prayer to Our Lady, Mother of Sorrows
Mary, Mother of Sorrows,
by the bitter martyrdom of the cross
and the agony of your Son,
remember with pity
the children of your sorrow:
aided by your prayers,
may we pass from death to life
and gain the crown of paradise.

Mother of grace, O Mary blest,
Mother of mercy tenderest,
Protect us when the foe is nigh,
And help us when we come to die.

Eastertide

The Easter Song of Praise (The Exsultet)
Rejoice, heavenly powers! Sing, choirs of angels!
Exult, all creation around God's throne!
Jesus Christ, our King, is risen!
Sound the trumpet of salvation!

Rejoice, O earth, in shining splendour,
radiant in the brightness of your King!
Christ has conquered! Glory fills you!
Darkness vanishes for ever!

Heavenly Father,
you have delivered us from the power of darkness,
and brought us into the kingdom of your Son:
grant that, as his death has recalled us to life,
so his continual presence in us
may raise us to eternal joy,
through Jesus Christ our Lord. *Amen.*

An Easter Sequence from the Byzantine Rite
Let God arise and let his enemies be scattered:
let them also that hate him flee before him.
> *Christ is risen from the dead!*
> *Death by death he doth downtread;*
> *And on those whom Death hath slain*
> *He bestoweth Life again.*

As smoke vanisheth, so shalt thou drive them away:
and as wax melteth at the fire, so let the wicked
perish at the presence of God.
> *Christ is risen ...*

But let the righteous be glad and rejoice before God:
let the poor and meek of the earth also be merry and joyful.
> *Christ is risen ...*

For this is the day which the Lord hath made:
let us rejoice and be glad in it. Alleluia!
> *Christ is risen ...*

Nailed to the Cross of your own free will,
O compassionate One;
laid in the grave as dead, O Life-giver;
destroying by death the dominion of death,
O Mighty One,
before you the gates of hell yawned open,
but you have raised those that were dead
since the beginning of time,
O lover of humanity.
Wherefore we glorify you
praising your resurrection
Jesus Christ our King,
God, for ever and ever.

An Easter Acclamation
It is our duty and our joy
that we should at all times
and in all places
give thanks to you,
O Lord God almighty,
because for the salvation of the human race,
your Son, Jesus Christ, suffered death on the cross;
whom Abraham prefigured in the offering of his Son,
and Moses foreshadowed in the offering of
A Spotless Lamb.
This is that Passover in which your faithful people rejoice.
O mystery full of devotion! O inexpressible and divine gift!
To ransom those in captivity
Christ gave himself to death at our hands.
But by his death he has destroyed death
and we, led forth from destruction,
and ascending to the realms of heaven
offer our praise and adoration.

A Litany of the Resurrection

Lord, have mercy.

Christ, have mercy.

Lord, have mercy.

O Christ, hear us.

O Christ, graciously hear us.

O God, the Father of heaven, R/ *Have mercy upon us.*

O God, the Son, Redeemer of the world

O God, the Holy Spirit

Holy Trinity, one God

Jesus, our Paschal Lamb offered for the sins of the world

Jesus, the first fruits of those that sleep, over whom death has no more dominion

Jesus, the Second Adam by whom came the resurrection from the dead

Jesus, who are yourself the resurrection and the life

Jesus, who laid down your life for the sheep

Jesus, who brought us life, immortality and light

Jesus, declared to be the Son of God with power

Jesus, the first-born from the dead, and ruler of the kings of the earth

Jesus, the First and the Last, who lives and was dead, and lives for evermore

Jesus, who rose early on the first day of the week

Jesus, who appeared to Mary Magdalene while it was still dark

Jesus, who sent angels to tell women that you were risen, as you had said

Jesus, with the disciples on the road to Emmaus, known in the breaking of the bread

Jesus, appearing to the twelve and greeting them with peace

Jesus, opening their minds to understand the scriptures

Jesus, breathing on the disciples to give them the Holy Spirit

Jesus, confirming the faith of Thomas by showing him your hands and side

Jesus, restoring Peter at the Sea of Tiberias, commissioning him to feed your sheep

By your glorious Resurrection, good Lord, deliver us.

By your victory over death, good Lord, deliver us.

By the glorious majesty of your risen life, good Lord, deliver us.

Lamb of God, you take away the sins of the world, have mercy on us.

Lamb of God, you take away the sins of the world, have mercy on us.

Lamb of God, you take away the sins of the world, grant us peace.

O God,
each year you gladden our hearts
by the celebration of the resurrection of
your Son Jesus Christ from the dead;
may we, who celebrate
these joyful days on earth
attain hereafter the eternal joys of heaven,
through the same Christ our Lord. *Amen.*

Easter and the Marriage Feast

In you, risen Jesus, God has shown us himself.
The gates of hell are shattered,
those already dead rise to life,
and now your promise has been fulfilled.
Easter is our marriage ceremony.
At Easter, you make us your brides,
sealing the union with your Spirit.

Sovereign Christ,
stretch out your strong hands over your whole Church
and over all your faithful people.
Defend, protect, and preserve them,
fight and do battle for them,
subdue the invisible powers that oppose them.
Raise now the sign of victory over us
and grant that we may sing the song of triumph
to your glory for ever and ever.   (St Hippolytus)

An Antiphon for Ascension Day

O King of Glory, Lord of Hosts,
the Victor who today ascended above the heavens;
leave us not comfortless
but send us the Promised of the Father,
the Spirit of Truth. Alleluia.

An Ascension Acclamation

It is our duty and our joy
that we should at all times
and in all places
give thanks to you,
O Lord God almighty,
because the Lord Jesus, the king of glory,
the conqueror of sin and death
ascended to heaven while the angels sang his praises.

Christ, the Mediator

between God and humanity,
judge of the world and Lord of all,
has passed beyond our sight,
not to abandon us but to be our hope.
Christ is the beginning, the head of the Church;
where he has preceded us in glory,
there we are called in hope.

An Ascensiontide Collect
O God, the King of Glory,
grant that as you have exalted
your only Son, Jesus Christ,
with great triumph to your heavenly kingdom,
so may we also know his presence with us,
according to his promise, to the end of time,
who lives and reigns with you
in the unity of the Holy Spirit,
one God, for ever and ever. *Amen.*

A Pentecost Antiphon
Come, Holy Spirit, fill the hearts of your faithful people, and kindle in us the fire
of your love. From the many races on the earth you unite your people in the
proclamation with one voice of the gospel of peace. Alleluia.

Send forth your spirit, O Lord:
And renew the face of the earth. Alleluia.

O God,
forasmuch as without you we cannot please you,
mercifully grant that your Holy Spirit may in all things
direct and rule our hearts;
through Jesus Christ our Lord. *Amen*

When the most high,
descending,
confounded the tongues,
he divided the nations;
when he distributed the tongues of fire
he called all peoples into unity;
therefore
with one voice
we glorify the most Holy Spirit:
Be thou exalted, O Lord, in thy Power.
We will praise and magnify thy mighty acts.
O blessed Paraclete, save us, who sing to thee:
ALLELUIA!
AMEN!

(Byzantine Liturgy)

O divine Love,
sacred Link,
uniting the Father and the Son,
almighty Spirit,
faithful Comforter of the afflicted:
penetrate the depth of my heart and will
with the brightness of thy light.
Send upon this desert, which is my soul,
the sparkling dew of thy grace,
and make fruitful that which has long been barren.
Let the fiery darts of thy love
reach the sanctuary of my soul and,
entering therein, set it on fire
with so bright a flame
that all my weakness, neglect and languor
may be consumed in the passion
of thy gentle embrace.   (*St Augustine*)

For other devotions to the Holy Spirit, see *Devotions to Foster Prayer*, above p. 21.

DEVOTION TO MARY AND THE SAINTS

The Rosary

In this form of prayer we reflect on sets of 'mysteries', five aspects of the gospel
gathered under the heading of a simple theme.
The three traditional themes of joy, sorrow, and glory have presented the redemptive
work of Jesus from the perspective of Mary his mother.
A fourth theme, light, has been promoted by Pope John Paul II. This presents sacra-
mental events in the gospel to be approached in the spirit of Mary's example:
treasuring and pondering them in our hearts.
A rosary is made of five sets of beads looped together in a chain. Each bead is held
while saying a prayer.
Introductory prayers are said on the chain of beads outside the loop:
The Apostles' Creed (holding the cross)
Our Father ... (on the single bead)
Hail Mary ... (once on each of the three beads)
Glory be ... (on the chain)

For each of the sets of five mysteries, the rosary provides

Our Father … (on the single bead)

Hail Mary … (once on each of the ten beads)

Glory … (on the chain)

The intention is that the prayers should form a quiet rhythm that absorbs the distractions of our minds, freeing them to encounter the central Mystery of Christian faith: Jesus Christ, who is God-with-us.

1 The Joyful Mysteries
Mary as Mother of God; these events are the cause of her rejoicing in the Magnificat.

The Annunciation	(Luke 1:26-38)
The Visitation	(Luke 1.39-56)
The Birth of Jesus	(Luke 2:1-9)
The Presentation in the Temple	(Luke 2:22-39)
The Finding in the Temple	(Luke 2:41-51)

2 The Sorrowful Mysteries
Mother of Sorrows, fulfilling Simeon's prophecy, 'A sword will pierce your soul too.'

The Agony in the garden	(Luke 22:39-46)
The Scourging at the pillar	(Matthew 27:26)
The Crowning with thorns	(Matthew 27.29-30)
The Carrying of the Cross	(Luke 23:26-32)
The Crucifixion	(Luke 23:33)

3 The Glorious Mysteries
Mary as Woman of Glory, receiving from her Son and her God the crown of life.

The Resurrection	(Luke 24:1-8)
The Ascension	(Luke 24:50-53)
The Descent of the Holy Spirit	(Acts 2:1-4)
The Assumption of Our Lady	(Luke 1:48-52)
The Coronation of Our Lady	(Revelation 12:1)

4 The Mysteries of Light
Mary as Woman of Faith, proclaiming, 'Do whatever he tells you.'

The Baptism in the Jordan	(Matthew 3:16-17)
The Miracle at Cana (marriage)	(John 2:1-12)
The Proclamation of the Kingdom of God (penance)	(Mark 1:15)
The Transfiguration (the Church)	(Luke 9:28-36)
The Institution of the Eucharist	(Luke 22:19-20)

The Litany of Our Lady

Lord, have mercy
Christ, have mercy
Lord have mercy
O Christ, hear us
O Christ, graciously hear us
O God the Father of heaven, *R/ Have mercy upon us*
O God, the Son, Redeemer of the world,
O God, the Holy Spirit,
Holy Trinity, one God,
Holy Mary, *R/ Pray for us*
Holy Mother of God,
Holy Virgin of virgins,
Mother of Christ,
Mother of divine grace,
Mother most pure,
Mother most chaste,
Mother inviolate,
Mother unstained,
Mother most lovable,
Mother most wonderful,
Mother of good counsel,
Mother of the Creator,
Mother of the Saviour,
Virgin most prudent,
Virgin most worshipful,
Virgin most renowned,
Virgin most mighty,
Virgin most clement,
Virgin most faithful,
Mirror of righteousness,
Seat of wisdom,
Cause of gladness,
Vessel of the Spirit,
Vessel of honour,
Vessel of devotion wondrous,
Mystic rose,
Tower of David,
Tower of Ivory,
House of gold,
Ark of the covenant,
Gate of heaven,
Morning star,

Health of the sick,
Refuge of sinners,
Consoler of the afflicted,
Help of Christians,
Queen of Angels,
Queen of Patriarchs,
Queen of Prophets,
Queen of Martyrs,
Queen of Confessors,
Queen of Virgins,
Queen of all Saints,
Queen conceived without stain,
Queen taken up to heaven,
Queen of the most holy Rosary,
Queen of Peace,
Our Lady of Walsingham,
Lamb of God, you take away the sins of the world, have mercy on us.
Lamb of God, you take away the sins of the world, have mercy on us.
Lamb of God, you take away the sins of the world, grant us peace.

Grant us Lord, we pray,
the joy of continued health of mind and body:
and through the intercession of Blessed Mary ever-virgin,
free us of this present sadness and fill us with eternal joy.
We ask this through Christ the Lord. *Amen.*

Other prayers to Our Lady

The Memorare *of St Bernard*
Remember, O most gracious Virgin, that never was it known
that any who fled to your protection, implored your help
and sought your intercession was left unaided.
Inspired by this confidence, we fly to you,
O Virgin of virgins, our Mother!
To you we come, before you we stand, sinful and sorrowful.
O mother of the incarnate Word, despise not our petitions,
but in your mercy, hear and answer us.

O Mary,
recall the solemn moment when Jesus, your divine Son,
dying on the cross, confided us to your maternal care.
You are our Mother, we desire ever to remain your devout children.
Let us therefore feel the effects of your powerful intercession
with Jesus Christ.
Make your name again glorious in this place (or in Walsingham)
once renowned throughout our land
by your visits, favours and many miracles.

Pray, O holy Mother of God,
for the conversion of England,
restoration of the sick,
consolation for the afflicted,
repentance of sinners,
peace to the departed.

O blessed Mary,
Mother of God,
Our Lady of Walsingham:
intercede for us.

All holy and ever-living God,
in giving Jesus Christ to be our saviour and brother,
you gave us Mary, his mother, to be our mother also;
grant, we pray you, that we may be worthy
of so great a brother and so dear a mother.
May we come at last to you,
the Father of us all,
through Jesus your Son. *Amen.*

What shall I call thee, O Full of Grace?
Heaven, for of thee arose the Sun of righteousness;
Paradise, for thou hast budded forth
the Flower of Immortality;
Virgin, for thou didst hold in thy embrace
the Son who is God of all:
Pray to him that he will save our souls.   (Byzantine Liturgy)

O holy Virgin,
in the midst of your glory
do not forget the sorrows of this earth.
Cast a merciful glance upon those
who are struggling with difficulties,
those who are suffering,
their lips pressed constantly against
life's bitter cup.
Have pity on those who love each other
and are separated.
Have pity on our rebellious hearts.
Have pity on those we love.
Have pity on those who weep,
on those who pray
on those who fear. *(Walsingham Pilgrims' Manual)*

The Sub Tuum Praesidium
Mother of God,
we fly to you,
our shade and shelter
on our pilgrim's way.
Look kindly on our prayers,
and turn not from us
in our time of need.
But free us
from the dangers that beset us
radiant and holy Virgin.

This is the oldest known prayer to Our Lady. It was written shortly after the Council of Ephesus in 431.

An Antiphon to Our Lady
Holy Mary,
help of those in need,
give strength to the weak,
comfort the sorrowful,
pray for God's people,
assist the clergy,
intercede for religious.
May all who seek your help
experience your unfailing protection.

The Litany of the Saints

Lord, have mercy
Christ, have mercy
Lord have mercy
O Christ, hear us
O Christ, graciously hear us
O God the Father of heaven, R/ *Have mercy upon us*
O God, the Son, Redeemer of the world,
O God, the Holy Spirit,
Holy Trinity, one God,

Holy Mary, R/ *pray for us*
Holy Mother of God,
Holy Virgin of virgins
St Michael,
St Gabriel,
St Raphael,
All holy angels and archangels,
St John the Baptist,
St Joseph,
All holy patriarchs and prophets,

St Peter,
St Paul,
St Andrew,
St John,
St James,
St Philip,
St Bartholomew,
St Matthew,
St Simon,
St Jude,
St Matthias,
St Barnabas,
St Luke,
St Mark,
All holy Apostles and Evangelists,
All holy disciples of the Lord,

All holy innocents,
St Stephen,
St Ignatius,
St Lawrence,
St Vincent,
St Alban,
St Pancras,
St Fabian and St Sebastian,
St John and St Paul,
St Cosmas and St Damian,
All holy martyrs,

St Sylvester,
St Leo,
St Gregory
St Augustine,
St Jerome,
St Martin,
St Nicholas,
St Anselm,
St Chad,
All holy bishops and confessors,
All holy doctors,

St Anthony,
St Benedict,
St Cuthbert,
St Bede,
St Dominic,
St Francis,
St Ignatius Loyola,
St Francis Xavier,
St John Vianney,
All holy priests,
All holy monks and hermits,

St Mary Magdalene,
St Agatha,
St Lucy,
St Agnes,
St Cecilia,
St Catherine,
St Anastasia,
St Teresa,
St Hilda,
All holy virgins and widows,
All holy women of God,

St Paulinus,
St Wilfrid,
St Edward Confessor,
St Edmund,
St George,
St David,
St Patrick,
St Petroc,
All holy saints of God,

Lamb of God, you take away the sins of the world, have mercy on us.
Lamb of God, you take away the sins of the world, have mercy on us.
Lamb of God, you take away the sins of the world, grant us peace.

O God,
whose nature is always to have mercy,
receive our humble prayer.
Though our sins enslave us,
yet may your compassion set us free;
through Jesus Christ our Lord. *Amen*.

A Calendar of Saint's Days

JANUARY

1	**Mary, Mother of God**
2	St Basil the Great & St Gregory Nazianzen, Bishops and Teachers (379 & 386)
12	St Aelred of Hexham, *Abbot* (1167)
13	St Hilary, *Bishop and Teacher* (367)
17	St Anthony of Egypt, *Hermit and Abbot* (356)
21	St Agnes, *Child martyr* (304)
24	St Francis de Sales, *Bishop and Teacher* (1622)
25	**The Conversion of St Paul**
26	St Timothy and St Titus, *Companions of St Paul*
28	St Thomas Aquinas, *Priest and Teacher* (1274)

FEBRUARY

5	St Agatha, *Martyr*
10	St Scholastica, *Religious, sister of St Benedict* (547)
14	St Cyril & St Methodius, *Missionaries* (869 and 885)
23	St Polycarp, *Bishop and Martyr* (c.155)

MARCH

1	St David, *Bishop, Patron of Wales* (c.601)
2	St Chad, *Bishop and Missionary* (672)
7	St Perpetua & St Felicity, *Martyrs* (203)
17	St Patrick, *Bishop, Missionary, Patron of Ireland* (c. 460)
19	**St Joseph**, *Guardian of the Holy Family*
20	St Cuthbert, *Bishop and Missionary* (687)
25	**The Annunciation of Our Lord**

APRIL

21	St Anselm, *Bishop and Teacher* (1109)
23	**St George**, *Patron of England*
25	**St Mark**, *Evangelist*
29	St Catherine of Siena, *Religious and Teacher* (1380)

MAY

1	**St Philip & St James**, *Apostles*
2	St Athanasius, Bishop and Teacher (373)
14	**St Matthias**, *Apostle*
19	St Dunstan, Bishop (988)
25	St Bede, Monk and Scholar (735)
26	St Augustine of Canterbury, Bishop and Missionary (605)
31	**The Visitation of The Blessed Virgin Mary**

JUNE

1	St Justin, Martyr (c.165)
5	St Boniface, Bishop, Missionary, Martyr (754)
9	St Columba, Abbot and Missionary (597)
11	**St Barnabas**, *Apostle*
13	St Anthony of Padua, Priest and Teacher (1231)
16	St Richard of Chichester, Bishop (1253)
22	St Alban, First Martyr of Britain (c. 250)
24	**Birthday of St John the Baptist**
28	St Irenaeus, Bishop and Teacher (c.200)
29	**St Peter & St Paul**, *Apostles*

JULY

3	**St Thomas**, *Apostle*
11	St Benedict, Abbot (c.550)
15	St Bonaventure, Bishop and Teacher (1274)
	St Swithun, Bishop (c.862)
22	St Mary Magdalene
25	**St James**, *Apostle*
26	St Joachim & St Anne, *Parents of the Blessed Virgin Mary*
29	St Martha

Devotions for the *Seasons* and the *Saints*

AUGUST

1	St Alphonsus de Liguori, *Bishop and Teacher* (1787)
4	St John Vianney, *Priest* (1859)
6	**The Transfiguration of the Lord**
8	St Dominic, *Priest and Founder of the Order of Preachers* (1221)
10	St Laurence, *Deacon and Martyr* (258)
11	St Clare, *Founder of the Poor Clares* (1253)
15	**The Assumption of the Blessed Virgin Mary**
20	St Bernard, *Abbot* (1153)
24	**St Bartholomew**, *Apostle*
27	St Monica, *Mother of St Augustine* (387)
28	St Augustine, *Bishop and Doctor* (430)
29	Beheading of St John the Baptist
31	St Aidan, *Bishop and Missionary* (651)

SEPTEMBER

3	St Gregory the Great, *Bishop and Teacher* (604)
8	**The Birthday of the Blessed Virgin Mary**
13	St John Chrysostom, *Bishop and Teacher* (407)
14	**The Exaltation of the Holy Cross**
15	St Cyprian, *Bishop and Martyr* (258)
21	**St Matthew**, *Apostle and Evangelist*
27	St Vincent de Paul, *Priest and Reformer* (1660)
28	**St Michael and All Angels**
30	St Jerome, *Priest and Scholar* (420)

OCTOBER

4	St Francis of Assisi, *Religious and Founder of the Friars Minor* (1226)
13	St Edward Confessor, *King of England* (1066)
15	St Teresa of Avila, *Teacher and Reformer* (1582)
17	St Ignatius of Antioch, *Bishop and Martyr* (c. 107)
18	**St Luke**, *Evangelist*
28	**St Simon & St Jude**, *Apostles*

NOVEMBER

1	**All Saints**
2	**All Souls**
10	St Leo the Great, Bishop and Teacher (461)
11	St Martin of Tours, Bishop (c. 397)
18	St Hugh of Lincoln, Bishop (1200)
17	St Elizabeth of Hungary, Religious (1231)
19	St Hilda of Whitby, Abbess (680)
20	St Edmund, King and Martyr (870)
22	St Cecilia, Martyr and Patroness of Musicians
23	St Clement of Rome, Bishop and Martyr (c.100)
30	St Andrew, Apostle and Patron of Scotland

DECEMBER

6	St Nicholas, Bishop (c.326)
7	St Ambrose, Bishop and Teacher (397)
8	**The Immaculate Conception of the Blessed Virgin Mary**
13	St Lucy, Martyr (304)
14	St John of the Cross, Priest and Teacher (1591)
25	**CHRISTMAS DAY**
26	**St Stephen**, Deacon and First Martyr
27	**St John**, Apostle and Evangelist
28	**The Holy Innocents**
29	St Thomas Becket, Bishop and Martyr (1170)

Devotions for the Seasons and the Saints

Prayers for Saints' Days

Feasts of the Blessed Virgin Mary
Almighty and everlasting God,
who stooped to raise fallen humanity
through the child-bearing of blessed Mary;
grant that we, who have seen your glory
revealed in our human nature
and your love made perfect in our weakness,
may daily be renewed in your image
and conformed to the pattern of your Son,
Jesus Christ our Lord,
who is alive and reigns with you,
in the unity of the Holy Spirit,
one God, now and for ever. *Amen.*   (*Common Worship*)

Feasts of Apostles and Evangelists
Almighty God,
who built your Church upon the foundation
of the apostles and prophets,
with Jesus Christ himself as the chief cornerstone:
so join us together in unity of spirit by their doctrine,
that we may be made a holy temple acceptable to you;
through Jesus Christ our Lord. *Amen.*

Feasts of Martyrs
Almighty God,
by whose grace and power you holy martyr(s) N.
triumphed over suffering and was faithful unto death:
strengthen us with your grace,
that we may endure reproach and persecution
and faithfully bear witness to the name
of Jesus Christ our Lord. *Amen.*   (*Common Worship*)

Feasts of Teachers of the Faith

Almighty God,
who enlightened your Church
by the teaching of your servant N:
enrich it evermore with your heavenly grace
and raise up faithful witnesses
who, by their life and teaching,
may proclaim the truth of your salvation;
through Jesus Christ our Lord. *Amen.*

(Common Worship)

Feasts of Bishops

Almighty God,
the light of the faithful and shepherd of souls,
who set your servant N. to be a bishop in the Church,
to feed your sheep by the word of Christ
and to guide them by good example:
give us grace to keep the faith of the Church
and to follow in the footsteps
of Jesus Christ our Lord. *Amen*

(Common Worship)

Feasts of Religious

Almighty God,
by whose grace N, kindled with the fire of your love,
became a burning and a shining light in the Church:
inflame us with the same spirit of discipline and love,
that we may ever walk before you as children of light;
through Jesus Christ our Lord. *Amen.*

(Common Worship)

Feasts of Missionaries
Everlasting God,
whose servant N carried the good news of your Son
(to the people of ...);
grant that we who commemorate that witness to the faith
may bear the glory of the gospel in our hearts
and manifest its light in all our ways;
through Jesus Christ our Lord. *Amen.*

(Common Worship)

Feasts of any Saint

Almighty Father,
you have built up your Church
through the love and devotion of your saints:
inspire us to follow the example of N,
whom we commemorate today,
that we in our generation may rejoice
with the company of heaven
in the vision of your glory;
through Jesus Christ our Lord. *Amen.*

(Common Worship)

Almighty God,
you have knit together your elect
in one communion and fellowship
in the mystical body of your Son
Christ our Lord:
grant us grace so to follow your blessed saints
in all virtuous and godly living
that we may come to those inexpressible joys
that you have prepared for those who truly love you;
thorough Jesus Christ our Lord. *Amen*

(Common Worship)

For a Christian ruler:
Sovereign God,
you set N over your people to be a ruler,
with grace to serve them humbly;
help us to follow this example of service,
to advance your kingdom on earth
and to enjoy its fullness in heaven;
through Jesus Christ our Lord. *Amen.*   (Common Worship)

Of the angels:
Everlasting God,
you have ordained and constituted
the ministry of angels and mortals
in a wonderful order:
grant that as your angels always
serve you in heaven,
so, at your command,
they may help and defend us on earth,
through Jesus Christ our Lord. *Amen.*   (Common Worship)

Of St Joseph:
God our Father,
who from the family of your servant David
raised up Joseph the carpenter
to be the guardian of your incarnate Son
and husband of the Blessed Virgin Mary:
give us grace to follow him
in faithful obedience to your commands;
through Jesus Christ our Lord. *Amen.*   (Common Worship)

Of St John the Baptist:
God our Father,
you called John the Baptist
to be the herald of your Son's birth and death.
As he gave his life in witness to truth and justice,
so may we strive to profess our faith in your gospel;
through Jesus Christ our Lord. *Amen.*   (Common Worship)

Of the faithful departed:
Eternal God, our maker and redeemer,
grant us, with all the faithful departed,
the sure benefits of your Son's saving passion
and glorious resurrection,
that, on the last day,
when you gather up all things in Christ,
we may with them enjoy the fullness
of your promises;
through Jesus Christ our Lord. *Amen.*   (Common Worship)

PENITENTIAL DEVOTIONS

Then I said, 'Woe is me! I am lost, for I am a man of unclean lips and I live among a people of unclean lips, and my eyes have seen the King, the Lord of hosts!' (Isaiah 6:5)

Come to me all you who labour and are overburdened, and I will give you rest.

(Matthew 11.28)

Penitence should be a quality in Christian living that is unrestrained, joyful and life-changing.

This quality will be evoked by a variety of experiences. Perhaps the most immediate will be the heart-stabbing pain of confronting our own responsibility for causing suffering, fear, and alienation.

But, as Isaiah's vision reminds us, penitence is also a response to the vision of the majesty of God, together with 'the unwelcome fact of our presence in other people's histories' (Rowan Williams) that pinpoints sin in social structures and relationships.

In order to avoid the destructive impact of guilt (how easily we can become 'confident in self-despair', as Charles Wesley puts it) it is important that we allow Jesus to minister to us by lifting the burden of our self-containment and comfortable self-importance.

The devotions that follow are suitable for use in two situations. The first is routine, in the recognition of sin and forgiveness that should be part of the fabric of life.

The second is particular: response to an event or situation in which you need to seek reconciliation. You may undertake that process through prayerful use of these devotions. They form the prelude to Confession.

In whatever form, penitence is the gateway to renewal in prayer and Christian action.

SELF-EXAMINATION: ADMITTING THAT THE FAULT IS YOURS

There is no great mystery to making your confession. But it does require courage to tell the story – your story – of the repeatedly shameful, silly, damaging, and, occasionally, the seriously evil things that you have done.

This story is a conversation between you and God. The priest is there as your friend and God's minister. Although a priest is instrumental in bringing about the sacramental encounter, the business is yours. That is why it is 'sealed', so that the priest may never mention it again.

Like you, the priest is also a penitent – human, sinful, and dependent on the grace of forgiveness. And therefore never shocked, or judgemental: simply a common traveller to whom is entrusted the stewardship of speaking the word of God's forgiveness.

As you prepare what you want to confess, remember to be specific (no names, just facts), simple in the telling (don't dress it up), and brief (that's the advantage of a list – you know when to stop!).

What are my sins? You sin by what you, and you alone intend to do, think or say, or deliberately refuse to do, think or say. You sin in relationship: with God, your family, your work, your neighbour (remember the story, 'And who is my neighbour ... '), and yourself.

How do I judge? The law of perfect charity is the standard God sets us. The conventions of the world often blur the demands of that law, and confession can be exploratory: 'This doesn't feel right, and I'm not sure; is it sinful, these days ...'

Where do I begin? With prayer, some time alone, possibly some tears, a fair amount of silence, and the Bible. And a pen and paper. And God. And his response: But I love you.

And the results? Forgiveness is freedom. Your intention is to change, to avoid the pitfalls and enjoy the freedom. It calls for a celebration.

The following prayers and scripture references may help in self-examination.

Come, Holy Ghost, our souls inspire,
And lighten with celestial fire;
Thou the anointing Spirit art,
Who dost thy sevenfold gifts impart:

Thy blessed unction from above
Is comfort, life, and fire of love;
Enable with perpetual light
The dullness of our blinded sight:

Anoint and cheer our soiled face
With the abundance of thy grace:
Keep far our foes, give peace at home;
Where thou art guide no ill can come.

Teach us to know the Father, Son,
And thee, of Both, to be but One;
That through the ages all along
This may be our endless song,
            Praise to thy eternal merit,
            Father, Son, and Holy Spirit.

O Holy Spirit, pour your bright beams into my soul, that I may discern my sins as clearly as I shall see them when I stand before the judgement seat of Christ. You are our guide to lead us into all truth; show me the truth about myself. Teach me my sins and the state of my life in your sight. Show me how often and to what extent I have offended you, the wrong I have done to my neighbour and myself, and all my sins of omission. Let nothing hinder me from the confession of my faults before the minister commissioned to act in your name, and so grant me access to the well-spring of forgiveness and new life. *Amen*.

Almighty and everlasting God, you hate nothing that you have made and forgive the sins of all those who are penitent: create and make in us new and contrite hearts, that we, worthily lamenting our sins and acknowledging our wretchedness, may receive from you, the God of all mercy, perfect remission and forgiveness; through Jesus Christ your Son our Lord, who is alive and reigns with you, in the unity of the Holy Spirit, one God, now and for ever. *Amen*.

(Common Worship)

O King enthroned on high,
filling the earth with your glory:
holy is your name,
Lord God almighty.
In our sinfulness we cry to you
to take our guilt away,
and to cleanse our hearts and minds
that we may hear your healing word;
through Jesus Christ our Lord. *Amen*.

Penitential Devotions

The guidance of the Word of God

- The sin and repentance of King David: 2 Samuel 12:1-25.
- The preaching of Jonah: Jonah 3, 4.

- The Beatitudes, standards of Christian living: Matthew 5:1-12.
- The Gerasene madman: Mark 5:1-20.
- The woman who loved much: Luke 7:36-50.
- The woman taken in adultery: John 8:3-11.
- The parable of the prodigal son: Luke 15:11-32.
- The parable of the Pharisee and the tax collector: Luke: 18:9-14.
- The parable of the unforgiving debtor: Matthew 18:23-35.
- The parable of the two sons: Matthew 21:28-32.
- Forgiveness at the cross: Luke 23:33-43.

Short statements of contrition for prayerful repetition

Father, I have sinned against heaven, and before you, and am no more worthy to be called your son/daughter.

- I have gone astray like a sheep that is lost. O seek your servant, for I do not forget your commandments.
- Enter not into judgement with your servant, O Lord, for in your sight shall no one living be justified.
- God, be merciful to me, a sinner.
- Make me a clean heart, O God, and renew a right spirit within me.
- Show me your ways, O Lord, and teach me your paths.
- O God, meet me in pity, embrace me in love, and forgive me all my sins.

O Christ my God,
as if before your dreadful judgement seat,
where there will be no respect of persons,
even so, coming to your most holy altar,
I bring before you and your majestic angels
my unrighteousness, my sinful thoughts and deeds.
As the God of them that are penitent,
and as the Saviour of sinners, save me for your pity's sake:
that where sin has abounded there grace may yet more abound,
that I may glorify thee with your eternal Father
and your most holy, gracious, and life-giving Spirit,
for ever and ever. *Amen.*

(St Simeon the Meditative)

Thou bowest thy head, O Crucified Love,
as if to greet me even in death;
thou openest thine arms as if to embrace me.
In that embrace would I live;
and in that embrace do I desire to die. *Amen.*

(St Augustine)

Accept my confession, O most loving, most gracious Lord Jesus
Christ, on whom alone my soul trusts for salvation; grant me
contrition of heart, and give tears to my eyes, so that I may truth-
fully acknowledge my failings with penitence, humility, and purity
of heart. *Amen.*

A FORM OF SACRAMENTAL CONFESSION

Kneeling or sitting where the priest is hearing confessions, ask for a blessing:
Bless me, for I have sinned.

After the priest has given a blessing, you begin:
I confess to almighty God, to blessed Mary, ever-virgin, to all the saints, and to you, that I have sinned in thought, word, deed, and omission, by my fault, my fault, my most grievous fault, especially since my last confession, which was … ago:
Say how long it was since your last confession; if this is your first confession, say 'since my baptism'. Then tell the priest your sins, and conclude the prayer:
For these and all my other sins that I cannot now remember, I am very sorry, firmly resolve not to sin again, and humbly ask pardon of God, and of you, advice, penance, and absolution.

The priest will give you advice to encourage you in your resolve to make a new beginning, and a penance, a simple act that is a sign of your reparation and integration back into the company of the faithful. This informal instruction is followed by the prayer of absolution, blessing and dismissal.

Our Lord Jesus Christ, who has left power to his Church to absolve all sinners who truly repent and believe in him, of his great mercy forgive you your offences: and by his authority committed to me, I absolve you from all your sins, in the name of the Father, and of the Son, and of the Holy Spirit. Amen.

May the passion of our Lord Jesus Christ, the merits of the Blessed Virgin Mary and all the saints, whatever good you have done, or evil you have suffered, be to you now for the remission of sins, the increase of grace, and the reward of eternal life. Amen.

Thanksgiving after Confession

Psalm 103 Benedic, anima mea
My soul, give thanks to the Lord,
all my being, bless his holy name.
My soul, give thanks to the Lord
and never forget all his blessings.

It is he who forgives all your guilt,
who heals every one of your ills,
who redeems your life from the grave,
who crowns you with love and compassion,
who fills your life with good things,
renewing your youth like an eagle's.

The Lord does deeds of justice,
gives judgement for all who are oppressed.
He made known his ways to Moses
and his deeds to the children of Israel.

Prayers in Life and in Death

Part One: Living Prayer

The events of new life are perhaps among the most potent signposts to the closeness of the majesty of God. No parent could doubt, looking at a new child, that mystery, miracle, and majesty are traces of divine life in us.

The prayers in this section offer a few handles on life's course that might help you to lift to God the needs of those with whom your identity is intertwined; parents for children, grandchildren, spouses for each other, friends for loved ones.

At some points, the handles are fixed to sacramental experience, and may therefore accompany the Church's liturgy. Reminders of those moments, a prayer card or photograph kept in these pages, may help you to look back with thanks.

They can also help, if darker times come when hope is dimmed, to remember that God does not forget, or withhold his love. The image of God in us is the foundation of 'the dearest freshness deep down things' (Hopkins), and when, at the last, dawn from on high breaks upon us, the majesty will be seen again.

Birth and Childhood

Blessing of an expectant mother.

Priest: Our help is in the name of the Lord
            Who has made heaven and earth.

Let us listen to the Gospel of the Lord.
Then his disciples came to Capernaum; and when Jesus was in the
house he asked his disciples, 'What were you arguing about on the
way?' But they were silent, for on the way they had argued with one
another who was the greatest. He sat down, called the twelve, and said
to them, 'whoever wants to be first must be last of all and servant of
all.' Then he took a little child and put it among them; and taking it in
his arms, he said to them, 'Whoever welcomes one such child in my
name welcomes me, and whoever welcomes me welcomes not me but
the one who sent me.'   (Mark 9:33-37)

R/ The almighty has done great things for me.
My soul proclaims the greatness of the Lord,
my spirit rejoices in God my Saviour;
he has looked with favour on his lowly servant.
From this day all generations will call me blessed. R/

He has mercy on those who fear him,
from generation to generation.
He has shown strength with his arm
and scattered the proud in their conceit. R/

He has cast down the mighty from their thrones
lifting up the lowly.
He has filled the hungry with good things
and sent the rich away empty. R/

He has come to the aid of his servant Israel,
to remember his promise of mercy,
the promise made to our ancestors,
to Abraham and his children for ever. R/

Priest:
Heavenly Father, creator of all that is,
good and loving as no one else can be,
hear our prayers for N.
as she prepares for the birth of her child.
Protect her from danger,
comfort and strengthen her in labour,
and in the birth of new human life
reveal the beauty of your image in us.
We ask this in the name of Jesus the Lord. *Amen.*

A woman's prayer for her unborn child
O God,
in these nine months of womanly patience,
I have learned more than ever
to marvel at your creative plans and our part in them.
I rejoice that the fashioning of a baby
and the founding of a family requires the gifts
of body, mind and spirit which you have given to each of us.
Bless these days of waiting, of preparation, of tender hope. *Amen.*

(Rita Snowden – adapted)

A parent's thanksgiving
Gracious God,
by whose providence we are fearfully and wonderfully made,
who has looked upon us when we were yet imperfect
and in whose book all our members are written;
to your divine majesty I/we offer hearty praise and thanksgiving
for the life of this infant whom your hands have fashioned,
the fruit of our union, a new revealing of your image and likeness.
Through the grace of sacramental life in your holy Church
bring that likeness to perfection in the eternal glory of heaven,
where you live and reign for all eternity. *Amen.*

Parents' and grandparents' prayer
O Lord my God,
shed the light of your love on my/our (grand)child.
To my/our ears cries and gurgles are meaningless;
but to you they are prayers for your blessing and delight at your grace.
Let my/our (grand)child learn the way of your commandments.
May *he/she* live the full span of life, serving your kingdom;
in death, may *he/she* have the sure and certain hope of salvation.
I/we do not ask that *he/she* be wealthy, powerful or famous,
but poor in spirit, humble in action, and devout in worship. *Amen.*

(Johann Stark)

Bless my children with healthful bodies,
with good understandings,
with the graces and gifts of your Spirit,
with sweet dispositions and holy habits:
and sanctify them throughout
in their bodies, and souls, and spirits,
and keep them unblamable
to the coming of the Lord Jesus. *Amen.*   (Jeremy Taylor)

For the adoptive family of a child
O God of love,
you have made us your children by adoption and grace;
as N. becomes a member of this family
bind them together by your grace,
and give them wisdom, joy, and faith.
Together may they grow in your love
and live out your plan for their pilgrimage
to the heavenly home of all your children;
through Jesus Christ our Lord. *Amen.*　　　　　(*Common Worship – adapted*)

For a child with special needs
O God,
we give thanks for entrusting N
to the special care of N and N.
Give them and all who surround them
wisdom, courage and patience.
Strengthen them with unfailing love,
that N may grow up in security, dignity
and the enjoyment of your presence,
to enrich our lives and the lives of others
in ways beyond our imagining,
through Jesus Christ our Lord. *Amen.*　　　　　(*Common Worship – adapted*)

Learning and Discernment

A child's prayer at night
Matthew, Mark, Luke and John,
bless the bed that I lie on.
Before I lay me down to sleep
I give my soul to Christ to keep.

Four corners to my bed,
four angels there aspread,
two to foot and two to head,
and four to carry me when I'm dead.

If I go by sea or land,
the Lord has made me his right hand;
if any danger come to me,
sweet Jesus Christ, deliver me.

He's the branch and I'm the flower,
pray God send me a happy hour;
and if I die before I wake,
I pray that Christ my soul will take.

(Traditional)

For true learning
Almighty God,
give light to our understanding,
that we may enjoy the fruits of our efforts,
in work and in all we do,
which we offer to your Son Jesus Christ
in thanksgiving for the gift of our life. *Amen.*

(A Downside pupil – adapted)

Before an examination
Help me, Lord,
to keep my mind fixed on truth.
Help me to concentrate on what I have learned
and not to worry about anything else.
You, who know all things,
prompt my memory with the light of understanding
that I may make good use of what I have been taught,
and not let my knowledge go to waste.
Thank you for my ability such as it is:
help me to use to the full and to remember
that all your gifts of mind, body and spirit
are for your glory and the service of others. *Amen.*

(*Catholic Prayer Book*)

Thanksgiving for sport and fitness
Thank you, Lord,
for fitness and strength,
for the enjoyment they give.
Give me discipline in training
and wisdom in performance.
Let me play fairly and support my team.
When we win, prevent me from boasting;
when we loose, keep me from excuses.
In the determination with which I play
teach me faithfulness and give me courage
to follow your commandments
in the training for life eternal,
through Jesus Christ the Lord. *Amen.* (*William Barclay*)

Discerning God's Will
Teach us, good Lord, to be generous,
and to serve you as you deserve;
to give and not to count the cost;
to fight and not to heed the wounds;
to toil and not to look for rest;
to labour and not to ask for any reward,
save that of knowing that we do your will;
through Jesus Christ our Lord. *Amen.*

(St Ignatius of Loyola)

A Meditation on Christian Vocation
God has created me
   to do him some definite service.
He has committed some work to me
   which he has not committed to another.
I have a mission.
Whatever, wherever I am, I can never be thrown away.
If I am in sickness, my sickness may serve him.
He does nothing in vain.
He knows what he is about.
   He may take away my friends;
   He may throw me among strangers;
   He may make me feel desolate,
   make my spirits sink,
   hide my future from me –
still he knows what he is about.
Therefore I trust him.

(John Henry Newman)

For priestly vocations

Almighty God, give us priests:
to establish the honour of your holy name;
to offer the holy sacrifice of the altar;
to give us Jesus in the holy sacrament;
to proclaim the faith of Jesus;
to tend your sheep;
to seek the lost;
to give pardon to the penitent sinner;
to bless our homes;
to pray for the afflicted;
to comfort mourners;
to strengthen us in our last hour;
to commend our souls;
Almighty God, give us priests! *Amen.*   (Prayer of the Additional Curates' Society)

Prayer for monastic vocations

It is in the silence of our hearts, O Lord,
that your voice calls us gently from self-will
to the search for you in monastic vocation.
We thank you for this gift to your Church
and pray that many will hear and answer it
as they seek to witness to the
truth and love of your kingdom on earth.
Through Jesus Christ our Lord. *Amen.*   (St Benedict Prayer Book)

Marriage

For those preparing for marriage
Lord of love,
bless N and N in all the preparations for their wedding day.
Increase your love in their hearts,
now and throughout their life together,
through Jesus Christ our Lord. *Amen.*

(Common Worship)

Thanksgiving for marriage
Tender and loving God,
thank you for the sacrament of marriage,
for the joy of bodily union
and the extension of the human race.
May the lives of all who are married
be a pledge of your love in a broken world,
and a sign of our hope that you will draw us
from estrangement into unity,
from guilt to repentance and forgiveness,
and from despair to the eternal bliss of heaven;
through Jesus Christ our Lord. *Amen.*

(Common Worship – adapted)

A prayer when in difficulty
Lord God,
our love has been like a morning cloud,
like the dew that goes away early.
Have mercy on us; deliver us from judgement,
bind up our wounds and revive us,
through Jesus Christ our Lord. *Amen.*

(Common Worship – adapted)

Prayers in Life and in Death

Blessing of a Home

Priest: Peace to this house.
> And to all that live here.

Priest: The Lord be with you.
> And also with you.

All praise, glory and thanks to you, Lord God,
that in your goodness you have given this dwelling
to be a home for N and N and their family.
As your Son the Good Shepherd sought out Zachaeus,
bringing conversion to his heart and salvation to his house,
so may that same Shepherd of our souls abide in this home,
bestowing on all who live and visit here
the enrichment of his presence and the gift of his peace,
who lives and reigns with you, in the unity of the Holy Spirit,
one God, for ever and ever. *Amen.*

The priest blesses water, saying:
Lord,
may this water, ✝ blessed in your name,
be a sign of protection for those who live here,
for their home and for all within it.
Abide with them always, protect them from harm,
and send your angels to watch over them.
We seek this blessing in the name of Jesus Christ your Son. *Amen.*

The priest then sprinkles the people present and every room. Then follows the proclamation of the word of God.

R/ The Lord, the Most High, is our dwelling.
Whoso dwells in the shelter of the Most High
and abides under the shadow of the Almighty,
shall say to the Lord, 'My refuge and my stronghold,
my God, in whom I put my trust.' R/

For he shall deliver you from the snare of the fowler
and from the deadly pestilence.
He shall cover you with his wings
and you will be safe under his feathers. R/

There shall no evil happen to you,
neither shall any plague come near your tent.
For he shall give his angels charge over you,
to keep you in all your ways. R/

Gospel reading
Let us listen to the Lord as he speaks to us in the gospel of John: 'Those who have my commandments and keep them are the people who love me; and those who love me will be loved by my Father, and I will love them and reveal myself to them.' Judas, (not Iscariot) said to him, 'Lord, how is it that you will reveal yourself to us and not to the world?' Jesus answered him, 'Those who love me will keep my word, and my Father will love them, and we will come to them and make our home with them.'

(John 14:21-23)

Prayers may follow, especially for the family of the newly blessed home,
neighbours, and the local community, concluding with the Lord's prayer:
As the children of one Father in heaven,
let us pray in the words the beloved Son
gave us:
Our Father ...

The priest then gives a blessing:
May the Lord bless you and keep you.
Amen.

May the Lord make his face to shine upon you
and be gracious to you.
Amen.

May the Lord lift up his countenance upon you
and give you peace.
Amen.

And may almighty God bless you,
† the Father, and the Son, and the Holy Spirit,
now and always.
Amen.

Prayer for a house blessing
O God, make the door of this house wide enough to receive
all who need human love and fellowship and your mighty care;
and narrow enough to shut out all envy, pride and hate.
Make its threshold smooth enough to be no stumbling block
to children or to straying feet,
but rugged enough to turn back the tempter's power.
Make it a gateway to your eternal kingdom. *Amen.*

(Thomas Ken)

Part Two: Dying to Live

Illness is not a divine verdict, it is a symptom of the sinfulness of a fallen world. We might participate in that sinfulness through the misuse of our bodies, but, as the Book of Common Prayer reminded its users each day, "God desireth not the death of a sinner." God is the giver of life and wholeness.

When we encounter physical suffering and incapacity in illness we become a patient. That word is a variant of a similar one; passion, especially in the sense that it is used to describe the redemptive suffering of Jesus.

Suffering is not, of itself a good thing, but uniting 'patient' and 'passion' it can be the means whereby in Christ God draws forth from mangled, hurting matter, new beauty and experience of his love. So an Advent hymn[1] can speak of 'glorious scars'.

Your illness may bring you spiritual benefit in a way you can recognize. It may make you a quite remarkable channel of grace to others. It may also be the prelude to death, itself the gateway to eternal life.

The prayers that are offered here are intended to help sustain the patient/passion and to trust in God.

1 'Lo, He Comes with Clouds Descending.'

Some practical observations and encouragement

- If you are in hospital, remember that you will be witnessing to your faith by your cheerfulness, courtesy, courage, and the very act of saying of your prayers. Strive to express your gratitude to those who are caring for you.
- But also guard your conversation against destructive and unkind comments that pain can make so easy.
- Make a point of ensuring that the Chaplain knows you are a Christian and would like to be ministered to appropriately.
- Make sure that your parish priest knows you are in hospital, so that you can be prayed for and visited.

- If you are terminally ill, do your best to seek and bear the information about your death.
- Try to receive the news calmly and with good sense. You may need to set your affairs in order, to make a will, prepare your funeral, and ensure that those you love know you are preparing for the journey home to God.
- Prayer will be important. If you are on medication, it is likely to be simple but deep, probably using prayers only known by heart. You should have favourite prayers, scripture quotations or verses of hymns ready to use for this moment.
- If death is close, say what really matters to your family and friends. To tell them how you have loved them or to say sorry for anything that is on your conscience can be your most precious legacy. Pray with them.
- Ask for a priest who will come to bring assurance of God's forgiveness now that you seek it, to anoint you, and if you are physically capable, give you holy communion. The priest is also a personification of the community of the Church, by whose prayers you will be surrounded and borne to God.
- Be thankful for the gift of your life and God's mercies throughout it; be penitent for your sins and confident of forgiveness; think much on the joys of heaven.

Prayers in sickness

When in pain
God our Father,
turn our eyes to your Son,
our example of courage in suffering.
In his nailing to the cross we learn
that suffering can be turned to blessing.
We long for comfort and pleasure,
and turn from the torture of you Son,
his body wracked with pain.
Yet when we see him rise in glory
we perceive that nails which fixed him to the cross
were also used to fashion the gates of life eternal.
Give us grace to bear our suffering
in the certain knowledge of eternal bliss,
through Jesus Christ our Lord. *Amen.*   (François Fénelon)

Lord Jesus Christ,
you invited those who labour
and are overburdened to find rest beneath your yoke.
Look upon my suffering, a yoke I cannot bear alone.
Grant me your refreshment, fill me with the strength
of martyrs in their torments, do not let me fall into
temptation or despair, but anoint me with the balm
of your grace and peace. *Amen.*

Simple Acts of Devotion

Praise
>LORD LET ME PRAISE YOU FOR EVER,
>IN SICKNESS AS IN HEALTH.

Self-offering
>LORD, SANCTIFY MY CROSS TO ME,
>AND KEEP ME YOURS FOR EVER.

Trust
>LET NOTHING DISTURB YOU,
>NOTHING DISMAY YOU;
>ALL THINGS ARE PASSING:
>GOD NEVER CHANGES.
>PATIENT ENDURANCE
>ATTAINS ALL THAT IT STRIVES FOR;
>THOSE WHO HAVE GOD
>FIND THEY LACK NOTHING.
>GOD ALONE SUFFICES.

(Teresa of Avila)

GOD BE IN MY HEAD, AND IN MY UNDERSTANDING;
GOD BE IN MY EYES, AND IN MY LOOKING;
GOD BE IN MY MOUTH, AND IN MY SPEAKING;
GOD BE IN MY HEART, AND IN MY THINKING;
GOD BE AT MINE END, AND AT MY DEPARTING.

(Sarum Primer)

BLESSING AND HONOUR AND THANKSGIVING AND PRAISE,
MORE THAN WE CAN UTTER, MORE THAN WE CAN CONCEIVE,
BE YOURS, O HOLY AND GLORIOUS TRINITY, FATHER, SON,
AND HOLY SPIRIT, FROM ALL ANGELS, ALL PEOPLES,
ALL CREATURES, FOR EVER AND EVER. AMEN.

(Thomas Ken)

The priest greets the sick person and any others present and introduces the rite, before the prayers of penitence:

Lord Jesus, you healed the sick: Lord, have mercy.
Lord, have mercy.
Lord Jesus, you forgave sinners: Christ, have mercy.
Christ, have mercy.
Lord Jesus, you give us yourself to heal us
and bring us strength: Lord, have mercy.
Lord, have mercy.

May almighty God have mercy on us,
forgive us our sins,
and bring us to everlasting life.
Amen.

Gospel reading

Hear the words of the gospel according to Matthew.
When Jesus entered Peter's house, he saw his mother-in-law in bed with a fever; he touched her hand, and the fever left her, and she got up and began to serve them. That evening they brought to him many who were possessed with demons; and he cast out the spirits with a word, and cured all who were sick. This was to fulfil what had been spoken through the prophet Isaiah, 'He took our infirmities and bore our diseases.'   (*Matthew 8:14-17*)

---

1 Roman Ritual adapted, additional material from *Common Worship*.

The Prayers

Lord, look kindly on our sick *brother/sister*. R/   *Lord, hear our prayer.*

Give new strength in mind and body. R/

Ease all pain and suffering. R/

Free him/her from sin and temptation. R/

Sustain all who are sick with your power. R/

Assist all who care for the sick. R/

Give health to our brother/sister N

on whom we lay our hands in prayer. R/

The priest lays hands on the head of the person who is sick. Others may also lay hands at the same time.

The priest may pray silently or aloud:
In the name of God and trusting in his might alone,
receive Christ's healing touch to make you whole.
May Christ bring you wholeness
of body, mind and spirit,
and deliver you from every evil,
and give you his peace.
Amen.

The prayer over oil already blessed
Praise to you, God the almighty Father,
you sent your Son to live among us
and bring us salvation.
Blessed be God for ever.

Praise to you, God the only-begotten Son,
you humbled yourself to share our humanity
and you heal all our illnesses.
Blessed be God for ever.

Praise to you, God the Holy Spirit,
the Consoler, you heal our sickness
by your mighty power.
Blessed be God for ever.

Lord,
hear our prayer for N whom we anoint in your name.
Ease his/her sufferings and in weakness be his/her strength.
through Jesus Christ our Lord. *Amen.*

As the priest anoints the forehead:
Through this holy anointing
may the Lord in his love and mercy
help you with the grace of the Holy Spirit. *Amen.*

As the priest anoints the hands (on the palms):
May the Lord, who frees you from sin and death
save you and raise you up. *Amen.*

Or the priest may say:
N, I anoint you in the name of God who gives you life.
Receive Christ's forgiveness, his healing and his love.
May the Father of our Lord Jesus Christ
grant you the riches of his grace,
his wholeness and his peace. *Amen.*

Prayers after anointing
Father in heaven,
grant N comfort in his/her suffering.
When afraid, give him/her courage,
When afflicted, grant him/her patience,
when dejected, afford him/her hope,
and when alone assure him/her of
the prayerful support of your holy people,
through Jesus Christ our Lord. *Amen.*

The almighty Lord,
who is a strong tower for all who put their trust in him,
whom all things in heaven, on earth, and under the earth obey,
be now and evermore your defence.
May you believe and trust that the only name under heaven
given for health and salvation
is the name of our Lord Jesus Christ. *Amen.*

Jesus, who has shared our life and borne our infirmities
taught us to call God our Father, and so we pray:
Our Father ...

The priest concludes with a blessing.

Prayers as death approaches

The Nunc dimittis
Lord, now lettest thou thy servant depart in peace:
according to thy word.
For mine eyes have seen: thy salvation.
Which thou hast prepared: before the face of all people.
To be a light to lighten the gentiles:
and to be the glory of thy people, Israel.
Glory ...

Psalm 23
The Lord is my shepherd: therefore can I lack nothing.
He shall feed me in a green pasture: and lead me forth
in the paths of righteousness, for his Name sake.
He shall convert my soul: and lead me forth beside
the waters of comfort, for his Name's sake.
Yea, though I walk through the valley of the shadow of death,
I will fear no evil: for thou art with me; thy rod
and thy staff comfort me.
Thou shalt prepare a table before me against them that trouble me:
thou hast anointed my head with oil and my cup shall be full.
But thy loving-kindness and mercy shall follow me all the
days of my life: and I will dwell in the house of the Lord
for ever.
Glory ...

A prayer for use at the bedside
Lord Jesus Christ, here is that lost sheep
for whom you left the ninety-nine
and wandered in the wilderness.
Here is the one for whom you,
the Good Shepherd, laid down your life.
Receive, now, the defenceless one
whose only hope is in your mercy.
(Lord, hear our prayer.)

Lord Jesus Christ, here is that traveller
who has fallen among thieves
and received many blows and injuries.
You are the physician of souls, our Good Samaritan;
in the last hour of this pilgrim take pity
and open the gates of refuge to one who trusts in you.
(Lord, hear our prayer.)

Lord, grant to our *brother/sister* N
and to us all a place with your saints
who from the beginning of the world
have served you in their several generations;
together let us rejoice in your sight for ever.
Amen.

Commendation

At the time of death, or when it is near

Go forth upon your journey, Christian soul:
go from this world
in the name of God the Father who created you,
in the name of Jesus Christ, who suffered for you,
in the name of the Holy Spirit, who was poured upon you,
in communion with Mary, and all the saints,
with angels and archangels and all the heavenly host.
May peace be yours this day,
and your home the heavenly Jerusalem. *Amen.*

N, our companion in faith and *brother/sister* in Christ,
we entrust you to God who created you.
May you return to him
who formed you from the dust of the earth.
May holy Mary, the angels, and all the saints
come to meet you as you go forth from this life.
May Christ who was crucified for you
bring you freedom and peace.
May Christ who died for you
admit you into the garden of paradise.
May Christ, the Good Shepherd,
give you a place within his flock.
May Christ forgive you your sins
and set you among his people.
May you see your Redeemer face to face,
and enjoy the vision of God for ever. *Amen.*

May the angels lead you into paradise
the martyrs welcome you as you draw near
and lead you into Jerusalem the heavenly City.
May choirs of angels welcome you, and there,
where Lazarus is poor no longer,
may you have eternal rest.

✝ Rest eternal grant to N, O Lord,
and let light perpetual shine upon *him/her*.
May *he/she* rest in peace; and rise in glory. *Amen.*

For those who mourn
Almighty God,
Father of all mercies and giver of all comfort:
deal graciously, we pray, with those who mourn,
that, casting all their care on you,
they may know the consolation of your love;
through Jesus Christ our Lord. *Amen.*   (Order for Funerals)

After a suicide
God of compassion,
forgive the despair of N for whom we pray.
Heal in *him/her* that which is broken
and in your love minister to those
hurt by the violence of *his/her* end.
Receive N into the kingdom where
by your mercy, we sinners also seek a place,
through the merits of Jesus Christ,
our wounded healer and redeemer. *Amen.*   (Common Worship – adapted)

For one who died young
God of all mystery,
whose ways are beyond understanding,
as we grieve at the untimely death of N
bestow upon us deeper trust in your love.
Help us, through tears and pain to discern your hand at work.
Bring blessing out of grief,
even as you brought your Son Jesus Christ
through death into resurrection life.
And this we ask in the name of Jesus the Lord. *Amen.*

(*Common Worship – adapted*)

Parents' and grandparents' prayer at the death of a child
God of love and life,
you gave N to us as our (grand)son/daughter.
Give us now the assurance that,
though passed from our sight, N has not passed from your care.
Be close to us in our sadness, and bring blessing out of grief.
Stay with us in our tears and pain, for you alone can heal us
and restore our hope, through Jesus Christ our Lord. *Amen.*

(*Common Worship – adapted*)

Bring us, O Lord, at our last awakening
into the house and gate of heaven,
to enter into that gate and dwell in that house
where shall be no darkness or dazzling, but one equal music;
no noise nor silence, but one equal possession;
no ends nor beginnings, but one equal eternity
in the habitations of your glory and dominion,
world without end. *Amen.*

(John Donne)

Prayers in Life and in Death

We seem to give them back to you, O God,
who gave them to us.
Yet, as you did not lose them in giving,
so do we not lose them by their return.
Not as the world gives, do you give, O lover of souls.
What you give you do not take away,
for what is yours is ours also, if we are yours.
And life is eternal and love immortal,
and death is only an horizon,
and an horizon is nothing,
save the limit of our sight.   (Bishop Brent)

Give rest, O Christ, to your servants with your saints,
where sorrow and pain are no more, neither sighing,
but life everlasting.

You only are immortal, the creator and maker of all:
and we are mortal, formed from the dust of the earth,
and unto the earth shall we return;
for so you did ordain when you created me, saying,
'Dust thou art, and unto dust shalt thou return.'
All we go down into the dust;
and weeping o'er the grave, we make our song:
'Alleluia, Alleluia, Alleluia.'

Give rest, O Christ, to your servants with your saints,
where sorrow and pain are no more, neither sighing,
but life everlasting.   (Russian Kontakion for the Dead)

A Pattern for Morning and Evening Prayer

'The Canticle of Praise, unceasingly hymned in heaven and brought into this world of ours by our High Priest Jesus Christ, has been faithfully continued by his Church throughout the ages.'
(Pope Paul VI)

When words fail us, the familiarity of a song can come to our rescue: in the trenches, between lovers, over a wakeful child, at a funeral, for the Olympic Games, or to express before God our deepest aspirations.

The daily Office is a canticle – a song, though often a spoken one. Its words are essentially scriptural. The psalms and other canticles that form its content echo into our own time that tradition of holiness in which Jesus himself was nurtured, and of which he became the new song of God's delivery of his people.

Sharing in this song
The simple pattern of Morning and Evening Prayer offered here may provide an introduction to the daily Office, a way of getting started. If so, the time may come for you to move to a fuller version, widely available in a variety of forms.

It may be, however, that this simple pattern provides a lighter form of the Office that remains useful in busy times, or as a more slender thread of devotion during travel or holidays.

For some, commitments will mean that a daily obligation is not possible, but here is a sequence to dip into, without worrying too greatly about where the liturgical seasons has got to. There may also be just small parts of this sequence that you wish to use in isolation; the intercessions or collects or psalmody. As always, the pattern is not prescriptive, but it offers material from which to create your own canticle of praise.

O sing to the Lord a new song, for he has done marvellous things. With his own right hand and with his holy arm have won for him the victory.
(Psalm 98)

1. MORNING PRAYER

Sunday

+ O Lord, open our lips,
and our mouth shall proclaim your praise.
(or)
May Christ, the bright Morning Star,
shed his peaceful light on all mankind.

The day draws on with golden light,
Glad songs go echoing through the height,
The broad earth lifts an answering cheer,
The deep makes moan with wailing fear.

For lo, he comes, the mighty King,
To take from death his power and sting,
To trample down his gloomy reign
And break the weary prisoner's chain.

Maker of all, to thee we pray,
Fulfil in us thy joy today;
When death assails, grant, Lord, that we
May share thy Paschal victory.

To thee who, dead, again dost live,
All glory, Lord, thy people give;
All glory, as is ever meet,
To Father and to Paraclete.

Psalm 95

O come, let us sing to the Lord; *
let us heartily rejoice in the rock of our salvation.

Let us come into his presence with thanksgiving *
and be glad in him with psalms.

For the Lord is a great God, *
and a great king above all gods.

In his hand are the depths of the earth, *
and the heights of the mountains are his also.

The sea is his, for he made it, *
and his hands have moulded the dry land.

Come, let us worship and bow down, *
and kneel before the Lord our Maker.

For he is our God, *
and we are the people of his pasture and the sheep of his hand.

Glory be ...

Scripture reading

From the rising of the sun to its setting my name is great among
the nations, and in every place incense is offered to my name, and
a pure offering; for my name is great among the nations, says the
Lord of hosts.

(Malachi 1:11)

Jesus said to the woman at the well, 'Woman, believe me, the hour
is coming when you will worship the Father neither on this
mountain nor in Jerusalem. You worship what you do not know;
we worship what we know, for salvation is from the Jews. But the
hour is coming, and is now here, when the true worshippers will
worship the Father in spirit and truth, for the Father seeks such as
these to worship him.'

(John 4:21-24)

The Gospel Canticle

+ Blessed be the Lord the God of Israel,*
who has come to his people and set them free.

He has raised up for us a mighty Saviour,*
born of the house of his servant David.

Through his holy prophets God promised of old*
to save us from our enemies,
    from the hands of all that hate us,

To show mercy to our ancestors,*
and to remember his holy covenant.

This was the oath God swore to our father Abraham:*
to set us free from the hands of our enemies,

Free to worship him without fear,*
holy and righteous in his sight
    all the days of our life.

And you, child, shall be called the prophet of the Most High,*
for you will go before the Lord to prepare his way,

To give his people knowledge of salvation*
by the forgiveness of all their sins.

In the tender compassion of our God*
the dawn from on high shall break upon us,

To shine on those who dwell in darkness and the shadow of death,*
and to guide our feet into the way of peace.
Glory ...

Prayers

Adoration:	The mystery of the word made flesh ...
Praise:	For the beauty of creation ...
	For the triumph of the resurrection ...
Penitence:	For submission to doubt and despair ...
	For reluctance to share the gospel ...
Petition:	For all who minister as bishops, priests, and deacons ...
	For the peace of the world ...
Thanks:	For the encouragement of the household of faith ...
	For enjoyment and relaxation ...

Our Father ...

Grant, O Lord, we beseech thee, that the course of this world may be so peaceably ordered by thy governance, that thy Church may joyfully serve thee in all godly quietness; through Jesus Christ our Lord. *Amen.*

Eternal light, shine into our hearts,
eternal goodness, deliver us from evil,
eternal power, be our support,
eternal wisdom, scatter the darkness of our ignorance,
eternal pity, have mercy upon us;
that with all our heart and mind and soul and strength
we may seek your face and be brought by your infinite mercy
to your holy presence, through Jesus Christ our Lord. *Amen.*

+ The Lord bless us, and preserve us from all evil, and keep us in eternal life. *Amen.*

Monday

+ O Lord, open our lips,
and our mouth shall proclaim your praise.
(or)
Come, Holy Spirit, gift of love,
and visit us with your salvation.

Come down, O Love divine,
Seek thou this soul of mine,
and visit it with thine own ardour glowing;
O Comforter, draw near,
Within my heart appear,
And kindle it, thy holy flame bestowing.

Let holy charity
Mine outward vesture be,
And lowliness become mine inner clothing;
True lowliness of heart,
Which takes the humbler part,
And o'er its own shortcomings weeps with loathing.

And so the yearning strong,
With which the soul will long,
Shall far outpass the power of human telling;
For none can guess his grace,
Till he become the place
Wherein the Holy Spirit makes his dwelling.

Psalm 90   *Domine, refugium*
Lord, you have been our refuge * from one generation to another.

Before the mountains were brough forth, or the earth and the
world were formed,* from everlasting to everlasting, you are God.

You turn us back to dust and say: *
'Turn back, O children of earth.'

For a thousand years in your sight are but as yesterday, *
which passes like a watch in the night.

You sweep them away like a dream; *
they fade away suddenly like the grass.

So teach us to number our days *
that we may apply our hearts to wisdom.

Glory be …

Scripture reading
O Lord, you know; remember me and visit me, and bring down
retribution for me on my persecutors. In your forbearance do not
take me away; know that on your account I suffer insult. Your
words were found, and I ate them, and your words became to me
a joy and the delight of my heart; for I am called by your name,
O Lord, God of hosts.   (Jeremiah 15:15-16)

Jesus said, 'Ask, and it will be given to you; search, and you will
find; knock, and the door will be opened for you. For everyone who
asks receives, and for everyone who knocks, the door will be opened.
In everything do to others as you would have them do to you; for
this is the law and the prophets. Enter through the narrow gate; for
the gate is wide and the road is easy that leads to destruction, and
there are many that take it. For the gate is narrow and the road is
hard that leads to life, and there are few who find it.' (Matthew 7:7-8,12-14)

The Gospel Canticle
+ Blessed be the Lord the God of Israel ... (see p. 146)

Prayers

Adoration:	For the mysterious wonder and beauty of nature ...
Praise:	For the revelation of the truth in Christ ...
	For the inspiration of artists, designers and performers ...
Penitence:	For the misuse of God's creatures ...
	For personal, social and international selfishness and greed ...
Petition:	That we may do our duty to God and neighbour ...
	For a greater trust in our future in God's hands ...
Thanks:	For the divine gift of life and its uniqueness ...
	For the promise of the vision of God ...

Our Father...

O God, whose never-failing providence ordereth all things both in heaven and earth; we humbly beseech thee to put away from us all hurtful things, and to give us those things which be profitable for us; through Jesus Christ our Lord. *Amen.*

Holy Spirit, as this day begins
waken me to your presence; waken me to your indwelling;
waken me to inward sight of you, and speech with you,
and strength from you; that all my earthly walk may awaken into song
and my spirit leap up to you throughout this day and always. *Amen.*

+ The Lord bless us, and preserve us from all evil, and keep us in eternal life. *Amen.*

Tuesday

+ O Lord, open our lips,
and our mouth shall proclaim your praise.
(or)
In the presence of the angels
I will bless you, O Lord.

Angel-voices ever singing
round thy throne of light,
angel-harps, for ever ringing,
rest not day nor night;
thousands only live to bless thee
and confess thee Lord of might.

Yea, we know that thou rejoicest
o'er each work of thine;
thou didst ears and hands and voices
for thy praise design;
craftsman's art and music's measure
for thy pleasure all combine.

Honour, glory, might and merit
thine shall ever be,
Father, Son, and Holy Spirit,
Blessed Trinity!
Of the best that thou hast given
earth and heaven render thee.

Psalm 34   *Benedicam Domino*
I will bless the Lord at all times; *
his praise shall ever be in my mouth.

My soul shall glory in the Lord; * let the humble hear and be glad.

O magnify the Lord with me; * let us exalt his name together.

I sought the Lord and he answered me *
and delivered me from all my fears.

Look upon him and be radiant, *
and your faces shall not be ashamed.

This poor soul cried, and the Lord heard me *
and saved me from all my troubles.

The angel of the Lord
encamps around those who fear him, * and delivers them.

O taste and see that the Lord is gracious; * happy the one who trusts in
him!

Fear the Lord, all you his holy ones, *
for those who fear him lack nothing.

Glory ...

Scripture reading
Besides this, you know what time it is, how it is now the moment for you
to wake from sleep. For salvation is nearer to us now than when we
became believers. The night is far gone, the day is near. Let us then lay
aside the works of darkness and put on the armour of light.   (Romans 13:11-12)

Jesus said, 'You are the salt of the earth, but if salt has lost its taste, how
can its saltiness be restored? It is no longer good for anything, but is thrown
out and trampled under foot. You are the light of the world. A city built on
a hill cannot be hid. No one after lighting a lamp puts it under the bushel
basket, but on the lampstand, and it gives light to all in the house. In the
same way, let your light shine before others, so that they may see your
good works and give glory to your Father in heaven.'   (Matthew 5:13-16)

The Gospel Canticle
+ Blessed be the Lord the God of Israel ... *(see p. 146)*

Prayers

Adoration:	God the Son, enfleshed and made lower than the angels
Praise:	For the joys of family and social life ...
	For the gift of intelligence and human learning ...
Penitence:	For bad laws and customs, and social injustice ...
	For the misuse of technology and science ...
Petition:	For peace-keeping forces and administration of justice ...
	For schools and universities ...
Thanks:	For our friends and all who enrich our life ...
	For the best in journalism and the media ...

Our Father ...

Almighty and eternal God,
who sent your only-begotten Son
that our eyes might see, our ears hear,
and our hands handle the Word of life, the everlasting Christ;
as we proclaim that he is Lord, may we joyfully believe
the message of the angels and the witness of the scriptures,
through him who lives and reigns with you and the Holy Spirit,
one God, for ever and ever. *Amen.*

Lord, lift up the light of your countenance upon us,
that in your light we may see light,
the light of your grace today, the light of your glory hereafter;
through Jesus Christ our Lord. *Amen.*

+ The Lord bless us, and preserve us from all evil, and keep us in
eternal life. *Amen.*

Wednesday

+ O Lord, open our lips,
and our mouth shall proclaim your praise.
(or)
Count us among your Saints, O Lord,
that we may praise you for ever.

The Church of God a kingdom is
Where Christ in power doth reign,
Where spirits yearn till seen in bliss
Their Lord shall come again,

Glad companies of saints possess
This Church below, above;
And God's perpetual calm doth bless
Their paradise of love.

An altar stands within the shrine
Whereon, once sacrificed,
Is set, immaculate, divine,
The Lamb of God, the Christ.

There rich and poor, from countless lands,
Praise Christ on mystic Rood;
There nations reach forth holy hands
To take God's holy food.

O King, O Christ, this endless grace
To us and all men bring,
To see the vision of thy face
In joy, O Christ, our King.

Psalm 66   *Jubilate Deo*

1 Be joyful in God, all the earth; *
 sing the glory of his name, sing the glory of his name.

2 Say to God, 'How awesome are your deeds! * Because of your great strength
 your enemies shall bow before you.

3 All the earth shall worship you, *
 sing to you, sing praise to your name.'

4 Come now and behold the works of God, *
 how wonderful he is in his dealings with the children of humankind.

5 He turned the sea into dry land;
 the river also they went through on foot; * there we rejoiced in him.

6 In his might he rules for ever;
 his eyes keep watch over the nations; * let no rebel rise up against him.

7 Bless our God, O you peoples; *
 make the voice of his praise to be heard;

 Glory …

Scripture reading
Remember these things, O Jacob, and Israel, for you are my servant; I
formed you, you are my servant; O Israel, you will not be forgotten by
me. I have swept away your transgressions like a cloud, and your sins
like mist; return to me, for I have redeemed you.   (Isaiah 44:21-22)

Jesus said, 'Those who love me will keep my word, and my Father will
love them and we will come to them and make our home with them.
I have said these things to you while I am still with you. But the
Advocate, the Holy Spirit, whom the Father will send in my name, will
teach you everything and remind you of all that I have said to you.'

(John 14:23, 25-26)

The Gospel Canticle
☩ Blessed be the Lord the God of Israel ... (see p. 146)

Prayers

Adoration:	God the Holy Spirit, the giver of life ...
Praise:	For the powers of life in nature and humankind ...
	For the life of the saints in heaven ...
Penitence:	For self-centred lives ...
	For the disunity of the Church...
Petition:	For the mission of all the baptised using their gifts ...
	For the spread of the gospel ...
Thanksgiving:	For the holiness we see in others ...
	For the dedication of the emergency services ...

Our Father ...

Lord God,
waken our hearts and minds this day, that we may perceive your will
and pour all we are into the doing of it; so that when the evening comes
you may close our eyes with your blessing upon servants who,
with all your saints, have been faithful in following the footsteps of your Son,
Jesus Christ our Lord. *Amen.*

O Lord,
We beseech thee mercifully to hear us;
and grant that we, to whom thou hast given a hearty desire to pray,
may by thy mighty aid be defended and comforted in all dangers and
adversities; through Jesus Christ our Lord *Amen.*

☩ The Lord bless us, and preserve us from all evil, and keep us in
eternal life. *Amen.*

Thursday

+ O Lord, open our lips,
and our mouth shall proclaim your praise.
(or)
From the rising of the sun to its setting,
great is your name, O Lord, among the nations.

From glory to glory advancing, we praise thee, O Lord;
Thy name with the Father and Spirit be ever adored.
From strength unto strength we go forward on Sion's highway,
To appear before God in the city of infinite day.

Thanksgiving and glory and worship, and blessing and love,
One heart and one song have the Saints upon earth and above.
Evermore, O Lord, to thy servants thy presence be nigh;
Ever fit us by service on earth for thy service on high.

Psalm 92   *Bonum est confiteri*
1 It is a good thing to give thanks to the Lord, *
   and to sing praises to your name, O Most High;

2 To tell of your love early in the morning *
   and of your faithfulness in the night-time;

3 Upon the ten-stringed instrument, upon the harp, *
   and to the melody of the lyre.

4 For you, Lord, have made me glad by your acts; * and I sing
   aloud at the works of your hands.

5 O Lord, how glorious are your works! * Your thoughts are very
   deep.

6 The senseless do not know, * nor do fools understand,

7 That though the wicked sprout like grass * and all the workers of
   iniquity flourish,

8 It is only to be destroyed for ever; *
   but you, O Lord, shall be exalted for evermore.

11 My eyes will look down on my foes, *
   my ears shall hear the ruin of the evildoers who rise up against me.

12 The righteous shall flourish like a palm tree, *
   and shall spread abroad like a cedar of Lebanon.

Glory …

Scripture reading
Give some of your food to the hungry, and some of your clothing to
the naked. Give all your surplus as alms, and do not let your eye
begrudge your giving of alms. Seek advice from every wise person and
do not despise any useful counsel. At all times bless the Lord God, and
ask him that your ways may be made straight and that all your paths
and plans may prosper.   (Tobit 4:16,18-19)

Then the righteous will answer him, 'Lord, when was it that we saw
you hungry and gave you food, or thirsty and gave you something to
drink? And when was it that we saw you a stranger and welcomed
you, or naked and gave you clothing? And when was it that we saw
you sick or in prison and visited you?' And the king will answer them,
'Truly I tell you, just as you did it to one of the least of these who are
members of my family, you did it to me.'   (Matthew 25:37-40)

The Gospel Canticle
+ Blessed be the Lord the God of Israel ... (see p. 146)

Prayers

Adoration:	Jesus in the Blessed Sacrament of the Altar and the hearts of his people ...
Penitence:	For lack of confidence in God's grace in us ... For our careless communions ...
Petition:	For growth in wisdom and discernment ... For courage to seek Jesus in the poor ...
Thanks:	For our baptism and those who taught us the faith ... For the heroic work of all caring and relief agencies ...

Our Father ...

Shine upon us, O Lord, thou one true light,
that we may behold thy beauty in creation,
thy mind in the everlasting Gospel,
thy hand both in our reproofs and blessings,
and thy presence in our gifts of bread and wine,
O Father, Son, and Holy Spirit,
God blessed for evermore. *Amen.*

O God,
forasmuch as without you we are not able to please you;
mercifully grant that your Holy Spirit may in all things
direct and rule our hearts; through Jesus Christ our Lord. *Amen.*

+ The Lord bless us, and preserve us from all evil, and keep us in
eternal life. *Amen.*

Friday

+ O Lord, open our lips,
and our mouth shall proclaim your praise.
or
Forbid it Lord, that I should boast
save in the cross of our Lord Jesus Christ.

All ye that seek a comfort sure
In trouble and distress,
Whatever sorrow vex the mind,
Or guilt the soul oppress.

Jesus who gave himself for you
Upon the cross to die,
Opens to you his sacred heart,
O to that heart draw nigh.

Ye hear how kindly he invites;
Ye hear his words so blest –
'All ye that labour come to me,
And I will give you rest.'

O Jesus, joy of saints on high,
Thou hope of sinners here,
Attracted to those loving words
To thee I lift my prayer.

Psalm 51   *Miserere mei, Deus*

1 Have mercy on me, O God, in your great goodness; * according to
  the abundance of your compassion blot out my offences.

2 Wash me thoroughly from my wickedness * and cleanse me from
  my sin.

3 For I acknowledge my faults * and my sin is ever before me.

4 Against you only have I sinned * and done what is evil in your sight;

5 So that you are justified in your sentence * and righteous in your
  judgement.

6 I have been wicked even from my very birth, *
  a sinner when my mother conceived me.

7 Behold, you desire truth deep within me *
  and shall make me understand wisdom in the depths of my heart.

Glory ...

Scripture reading

For your strength does not depend on numbers, nor your might on the
powerful. But you are the God of the lowly, helper of the oppressed,
upholder of the weak, protector of the forsaken, saviour of those
without hope.   (Judith 9:11)

Jesus called the crowd with his disciples, and said to them, 'If any
want to become my followers, let them deny themselves and take up
their cross and follow me. For those who want to save their life will
lose it, and those who lose their life for my sake, and for the sake of
the gospel, will save it. For what will it profit them to gain the whole
world and forfeit their life? Indeed, what can they give in return for
their life?'   (Mark 8:34-36)

The Gospel Canticle
+ Blessed be the Lord the God of Israel. . . (see p. 146)

Prayers

Adoration:	Jesus, who by his cross and passion redeemed us
Praise:	For the obedience of Jesus, even to death ...
	The Father for loving us while we were yet sinners
Penitence:	For indifference to our besetting sins ...
	For indifference to the pain of others ...
Petition:	For the peace of the world ...
	For the redemption of our age and civilization ...
Thanks:	For forgiveness each day ...
	For our parents and those who nurtured us ...

Our Father ...

Grant, O Lord,
that in your wounds we may find our safety,
in your stripes our cure, in your pain our peace,
in your cross our victory, in your resurrection our triumph;
and a crown of righteousness in the glories of your eternal kingdom.
Amen.

O God, who would fold both heaven and earth in a single peace:
Let the design of thy great love lighten upon the waste of our
wraths and sorrows;
and give peace to the Church, peace among nations, peace in
our dwellings,
and peace in our hearts; through thy Son our Saviour Jesus Christ.
Amen.

+ The Lord bless us, and preserve us from all evil, and keep us in
eternal life. *Amen.*

Saturday

+ O Lord, open our lips,
and our mouth shall proclaim your praise.
(or)
The almighty has done great things for me
holy is his name.

Alleluia, sing to Jesus,
His the sceptre, his the throne;
Alleluia, his the triumph,
His the victory alone:
Hark the songs of peaceful Sion
Thunder like a mighty flood;
Jesus out of every nation
Hath redeemed us by his Blood.

Alleluia, King eternal,
Thee the Lord of lords we own;
Alleluia, born of Mary,
Earth thy footstool, Heaven thy throne:
Thou within the veil hast entered,
Robed in flesh our great High Priest;
Thou on earth both Priest and Victim
In the Eucharistic Feast.

Psalm 119   *Lucerna pedibus meis*

105 Your word is a lantern to my feet * and a light upon my path.

106 I have sworn and will fulfill it, *
    to keep your righteous judgements.

107 I am troubled above measure; *
    give me life, O Lord, according to your word.

108 Accept the free-will offering of my mouth, O Lord, * and teach
    me your judgements.

109 My soul is ever in my hand, * yet I do not forget your law.

110 The wicked have laid a snare for me, *
    but I have not strayed from your commandments.

111 Your testimonies have I claimed as my heritage for ever; * for they
    are the very joy of my heart.

112 I have applied my heart to fulfil your statutes * always, even to
    the end.

Glory be ...

Scripture reading

On that day many nations shall come and say, "Come, let us go up to the
mountain of the Lord, to the house of the God of Jacob; that he may
teach us his ways and that we may walk in his paths." For out of Sion
shall go forth instruction, and the word of the Lord from Jerusalem.
He shall judge between many peoples, and shall arbitrate between
strong nations far away; they shall beat their swords into ploughshares,
and their spears into pruning hooks; nation shall not lift up sword
against nation, neither shall they learn war any more.   (Micah 4:2-3)

Jesus said, 'Come to me all you who labour and are overburdened, and
I will give you rest. Shoulder my yoke and learn from me, for I am
gentle and humble in heart, and you will find rest for your souls. Yes,
my yoke is easy and my burden is light.   (Matthew 11:28-30)

The Gospel Canticle
+ Blessed be the Lord the God of Israel ... *(see p. 146)*

Prayers

Adoration:	God the Trinity in whom all creation is held together
	God the Holy Spirit, drawing us into the divine life
Praise:	For the lowliness and faith of Our Lady, St Mary ...
	For the lives of the hidden saints among us ...
Penitence:	For neglect of our family and our friends ...
	For disregard of our own personal dignity ...
Petition:	For an increase of vocations to the priesthood ...
	For Christians engaged in politics and social action ...
Thanks:	For teachers and places of learning ...
	For rest and recreation ...

Our Father ...

O God, you have given us ears to hear your word,
and tongues to sing your praise;
free our hearts, that, like the Blessed Virgin Mary
we may be obedient to your word;
free our lips that we may also worship you in spirit and in truth,
through Jesus Christ our Lord. *Amen.*

Stir up, we beseech thee, O Lord, the wills of thy faithful people;
that they, plenteously bringing forth the fruit of good works,
may of thee be plenteously rewarded; through Jesus Christ our Lord.
Amen.

+ The Lord bless us, and preserve us from all evil, and keep us in
eternal life. *Amen.*

2. EVENING PRAYER

Sunday

+ O God, make speed to save us.
        O Lord, make haste to help us.

Glory ...   Alleluia. *(except in Lent)*

Jerusalem the golden,
With milk and honey blest,
Beneath thy contemplation
Sink heart and voice opprest.
I know not, O I know not,
What social joys are there,
What radiancy of glory,
What light beyond compare.

They stand, those halls of Sion
Conjubilant with song,
And bright with many an Angel,
And all the Martyr throng;
The Prince is ever with them,
The daylight is serene,
The pastures of the blessed
Are decked with heavenly sheen.

O sweet and blessed country,
Shall I ever see thy face?
O sweet and blessed country,
Shall I ever win thy grace?
Exult, O dust and ashes!
The Lord shall be thy part:
His only, his for ever,
Thou shalt be, and thou art!

The Habit of Holiness

Psalm 150 *Laudate Dominum*

1 (Alleluia!) (except in Lent)
  O praise God in his holiness; *
  praise him in the firmament of his power.

2 Praise him for his mighty acts; *
  praise him according to his excellent greatness.

3 Praise him with the blast of the trumpet; * praise him upon the
  harp and lyre.

4 Praise him with timbrel and dances; * praise him upon the
  strings and pipe.

5 Praise him with ringing cymbals; *
  praise him upon the clashing cymbals.

6 Let everything that has breath * praise the Lord. (Alleluia!)

Glory ...

Scripture reading

Hear, O Israel: The Lord is our God, the Lord alone. You shall love the Lord your God with all your heart, and with all your soul, and with all your might. Keep these words that I am commanding you today in your heart. Recite them to your children and talk about them when you are at home and when you are away, when you lie down and when you rise. Bind them as a sign on your hand, fix them as an emblem on your forehead, and write them on the doorposts of your house and on your gates. *(Deuteronomy 6:4-9)*

You have come to Mount Zion and to the city of the living God, the heavenly Jerusalem, and to innumerable angels in festive gathering, and to the assembly of the firstborn who are enrolled in heaven, and to God the judge of all, and to spirits of the righteous made perfect and to Jesus, the mediator of a new covenant, and to the sprinkled blood that speaks a better word than the blood of Abel. *(Hebrews 12:22-24)*

Jesus said, 'This is my commandment, that you love one another as I have loved you. No one has greater love than this, to lay down one's life for one's friends. You are my friends if you do what I command you. I do not call you servants any longer, because the servant does not know what the master is doing; but I have called you friends, because I have made known to you everything that I have heard from my Father. You did not choose me but I chose you. And I appointed you to go and bear fruit, fruit that will last, so that the Father will give you whatever you ask him in my name. I am giving you these commandments so that you may love one another.' *(John 15:12-17)*

The Gospel Canticle

+ My soul proclaims the greatness of the Lord,
        my spirit rejoices in God my Saviour;*
he has looked with favour on his lowly servant.

From this day all generations will call me blessed;*
the Almighty has done great things for me
        and holy is his name.

He has mercy on those who fear him,*
from generation to generation.

He has shown strength with his arm*
and has scattered the proud in their conceit,

Casting down the mighty from their thrones*
and lifting up the lowly.

He has filled the hungry with good things*
and sent the rich away empty.

He has come to the aid of his servant Israel,*
to remember his promise of mercy,

The promise made to our ancestors,*
to Abraham and his children for ever.

Glory ...

Intercessions

- That in the coming week we may proclaim Jesus as risen and with us ...
- For the use of creation to sustain all life in plenty, thankfulness and beauty ...
- In thanksgiving for those gone before us on the pilgrimage of faith ...

Our Father ...

O God, from whom all holy desires, all good counsels, and all just works do proceed; give unto thy servants that peace which the world cannot give; that both our hearts may be set to obey thy commandments, and also that by thee we being defended from the fear of our enemies may pass our time in rest and quietness; through the merits of Jesus Christ our Saviour. *Amen.*

Lord God,
when our world lay in ruins
you raised it up again
on the foundation of your Son's passion and death;
give us grace to rejoice in the freedom from sin
which he gained for us,
and bring us to everlasting joy;
through Jesus Christ our Lord. *Amen.*

+ The grace of our Lord Jesus Christ, and the love of God, and the fellowship of the Holy Spirit be with us all, evermore. *Amen.*

Monday

+ O God, make speed to save us.
O Lord, make haste to help us.
Glory be ...   Alleluia (except in Lent)

O Thou who camest from above,
The pure celestial fire to impart,
Kindle a flame of sacred love
On the mean altar of my heart.

There let it for thy glory burn
With inextinguishable blaze,
And trembling to its source return
In humble prayer, and fervent praise.

Jesus, confirm my heart's desire
To work, and speak, and think for thee;
Still let me guard the holy fire,
And still stir up thy gift in me.

Ready for all thy perfect will,
My acts of faith and love repeat,
Till death thy endless mercies seal,
And make my sacrifice complete.

Psalm 15   *Domine, quis habitabit?*

1 Lord, who may dwell in your tabernacle? * Who may rest upon
   your holy hill?

2 Whoever leads an uncorrupt life, * and who does the thing that
   is right;

3 Who speaks the truth from the heart, * and bears no deceit on
   the tongue;

4 Who does no evil to a friend; *
   and pours no scorn on a neighbour;

5 In whose sight the wicked are not esteemed, * but who honours
   those who fear the Lord.

6 Whoever has sworn to a neighbour * and never goes back on
   that word;

7 Who does not lend money in hope of gain, * nor takes a bribe
   against the innocent;

8 Whoever does these things * shall never fall.

Glory ...

Where shall wisdom be found? And where is the place of understanding? Mortals do not know the way to it, and it is not found in the land of the living. The deep says, 'It is not in me,' and the sea says, 'It is not with me.' It cannot be bought for gold, and silver cannot be weighed out as its price. God understands the way to it, and he knows its place. And he says to humankind, 'Truly, the fear of the Lord, that is wisdom; and to depart from evil is understanding.'

(Job 28:12-14,23,28)

Even if our gospel is veiled, it is veiled to those who are perishing. In their case the god of this world has blinded the minds of unbelievers, to keep them from seeing the light of the gospel of the glory of Christ, who is the image of God. For we do not proclaim ourselves; we proclaim Jesus Christ as Lord and ourselves as your slaves for Jesus' sake. For it is the God who said, "Let light shine out of darkness," who has shone in our hearts to give the light of the knowledge of the glory of God in the face of Jesus Christ.

(2 Corinthians 4:3-6)

Jesus rejoiced in the Holy Spirit and said, 'I thank you, Father, Lord of heaven and earth, because you have hidden these things from the wise and intelligent and have revealed them to infants; yes, Father, for such was your gracious will. All things have been handed over to me by my Father; and no one knows who the Son is except the Father, or who the Father is except the Son and anyone to whom the Son chooses to reveal him.'

(Luke 10:21-22)

The Gospel Canticle
+ My soul proclaims the greatness of the Lord ... *(see p. 169)*

Intercessions
- For the inspiration of the people of God by the Holy Spirit ...
- For all who work in communications, for its right and best use ...
- For the safety of travellers and all responsible for transport ...

Our Father ...

Assist us mercifully, O Lord, in these our supplications and prayers, and dispose the way of thy servants towards the attainment of everlasting salvation;
that, among all the changes and chances of this mortal life, they may ever be defended by thy most gracious and ready help; through Jesus Christ our Lord. *Amen.*

O Christ, my Lord, I pray that you will turn my heart to you in the depths of my being, where the noise of creatures is silenced and the clamour of my distracted thoughts is stilled; so might I find you always present, and remain with you for ever. *Amen.*

+ The grace of our Lord Jesus Christ, and the love of God, and the fellowship of the Holy Spirit be with us all, evermore. *Amen.*

Tuesday

✝ O God, make speed to save us.
O Lord, make haste to help us.

Glory be ...   Alleluia (except in Lent)

O gladsome light, O grace
Of God the Father's face,
The eternal splendour wearing;
Celestial, holy, blest,
Our Saviour Jesus Christ,
Joyful in thine appearing.

Now ere day fadeth quite,
We see the evening light,
Our wonted hymn outpouring;
Father of might unknown,
Thee, his incarnate Son,
And Holy Spirit adoring.

To thee of right belongs
All praise of holy songs,
O Son of God, Lifegiver;
Thee, therefore, O Most High,
The world doth glorify,
And shalt exalt for ever.

Psalm 46 *Deus noster refugium*

1   God is our refuge and strength, * a very present help in trouble;

2   Therefore we will not fear, though the earth be moved, * and
though the mountains tremble in the heart of the sea;

3   Though the waters rage and swell *
and though the mountains quake at the towering seas:

4   There is a river whose streams make glad the city of God, * the
holy place of the dwelling of the Most High.

5   God is in the midst of her; therefore shall she not be removed; *
God shall help her at the break of day.

6   The nations are in uproar and the kingdoms are shaken; * but
God utters his voice and the earth shall melt away.

7   *The Lord of hosts is with us; * the God of Jacob is our stronghold.*

8   Come and behold the works of the Lord, *
what destruction he has wrought upon the earth.

9   He makes wars to cease in all the world; * he shatters the bow
and snaps the spear and burns the chariots in the fire.

10 'Be still, and know that I am God; * I will be exalted among
the nations; I will be exalted in the earth.'

11 *The Lord of hosts is with us; * the God of Jacob is our stronghold.*

Glory ...

Scripture reading

Seek the Lord, all you humble of the land, who do his commands;
seek righteousness, seek humility; perhaps you may be hidden on
the day of the Lord's wrath.   (Zephaniah 2:3)

We speak God's wisdom, secret and hidden, which God decreed
before the ages for our glory. None of the rulers of this age
understood this; for if they had, they would not have crucified the
Lord of glory. But, as it is written, 'What no eye has seen, nor ear
heard, nor the human heart conceived, what God has prepared for
those who love him' – these things God has revealed to us through
the Spirit; for the Spirit searches everything, even the depths of
God.   (1 Corinthians 2:8-10)

When Jesus was alone, those who were around him along with the
twelve asked him about the parables. And he said to them, 'To you
has been given the secret of the kingdom of God, but for those
outside, everything comes in parables; in order that "they may look
but not perceive, and may listen, but not understand; so that they
may not turn again and be forgiven".'   (Mark 4:10-13)

Gospel Canticle
+ My soul proclaims the greatness of the Lord ... (see p. 169)

Intercessions
- For the persecuted Church, for courage and protection...
- For the world's displaced people to find a home and dignity ...
- For courage and sensitivity as messengers of the gospel ...

Our Father ...

O Saviour,
restrain our pride and enlarge our hope,
that with true humility we may enter
in the joy and simplicity of childhood
the kingdom of our Father,
where, with the Holy Spirit,
you live in endless love. *Amen.*

Lighten our darkness, we beseech thee, O Lord, and by thy great
mercy defend us from all perils and dangers of this night; for the
love of thy only Son, our Saviour, Jesus Christ. *Amen.*

+ The grace of our Lord Jesus Christ, and the love of God, and the
fellowship of the Holy Spirit be with us all, evermore. *Amen.*

Wednesday

+ O God, make speed to save us.
> O Lord, make haste to help us.

Glory ...   Alleluia (except in Lent)

Ye servants of God, your master proclaim
and publish abroad his wonderful name;
the name all-victorious of Jesus extol;
his kingdom is glorious, and rules over all.

God ruleth on high, almighty to save;
and still he is nigh, his presence we have;
the great congregation his triumph shall sing,
ascribing salvation to Jesus our King.

'Salvation to God who sits on the throne!'
let all cry aloud, and honour the Son;
the praises of Jesus the angels proclaim,
fall down on their faces, and worship the Lamb.

Then let us adore, and give him his right:
all glory and power, all wisdom and might,
all honour and blessing, with angels above,
and thanks never-ceasing, and infinite love.

Psalm 84   *Quam dilecta!*

1 How lovely is your dwelling-place, O Lord of hosts! *
   My soul has a desire and longing to enter the courts of the Lord;
   my heart and my flesh rejoice in the living God.

2 The sparrow has found her a house
   and the swallow a nest where she may lay her young; * at your altars,
   O Lord of hosts, my King and my God.

3 Blessed are they who dwell in your house! * They will always be
   praising you.

4 Blessed are those whose strength is in you, * in whose heart are
   the highways to Zion;

5 Who going through the barren valley find there a spring; * and
   the early rains will clothe it with blessing.

6 They will go from strength to strength, * and appear before God
   in Zion.

7 O Lord God of hosts, hear my prayer; * listen, O God of Jacob.

8 Behold our defender, O God; *
   and look upon the face of your anointed.

9 For one day in your courts * is better than a thousand.

10 I would rather be a doorkeeper in the house of my God * than
   dwell in the tents of ungodliness.

11 For the Lord God is both sun and shield; the Lord will give grace and
   glory; * no good thing shall he withhold from those who walk
   with integrity.

12 O Lord God of hosts, * blessed are those who put their trust in you!

Glory ...

The days are surely coming, says the Lord, when I will raise up for
David a righteous Branch, and he shall reign as king and deal
wisely, and shall execute justice and righteousness in the land. In
his days Judah will be saved and Israel will live in safety. And this
is the name by which he will be called: 'The Lord is our
righteousness.'

(Jeremiah 23:5-6)

Speak and act as those who are to be judged by the law of
liberty. For judgement will be without mercy to anyone who has
shown no mercy; mercy triumphs over judgement.   (James 2:12-13)

As Jesus sat at dinner in the house, many tax collectors and sinners
came and were sitting with him and his disciples. When the
Pharisees saw this, they said to his disciples, 'Why does your
teacher eat with tax collectors and sinners?' But when he heard
this, he said, 'Those who are well have no need of a physician,
but those who are sick. Go and learn what this means, "I desire
mercy not sacrifice." For I have come to call not the righteous but
sinners.'

(Matthew 9:10-13)

The Gospel Canticle

✝ My soul proclaims the greatness of the Lord ... (see p. 169)

Intercessions

- For the Church in place of conflict: for the peace of Jerusalem ...
- For all doctors, nurses, and ancillary and support staff ...
- For those who have no one else to pray for them ...

Our Father ...

O Lord,
we pray not that our path will be smooth
but that we may walk it faithfully without fear,
we pray not always to see the heights,
but that your light may direct our steps
to the city of your Saints and angels,
the heavenly Jerusalem,
through Jesus Christ our Lord. *Amen.*

Lord,
preserve your household the Church
with enduring holiness.
Through your protection
may it be free from harm
to serve you faithfully
in the work of salvation,
through Jesus Christ our Lord. *Amen.*

✝ The grace of our Lord Jesus Christ, and the love of God, and the
fellowship of the Holy Spirit be with us all, evermore. *Amen.*

Thursday

+ O God, make speed to save us.
O Lord, make haste to help us.

Glory …   Alleluia   *(except in Lent)*

Just as I am, without one plea
But that thy Blood was shed for me,
And that thou bidds't me come to thee,
        O Lamb of God, I come.

Just as I am, though tossed about
With many a conflict, many a doubt,
Fightings within, and fears without,

Just as I am, poor, wretched, blind;
Sight, riches, healing of the mind,
Yea all I need, in thee I find,

Just as I am, thou wilt receive,
Wilt welcome, pardon, cleanse, relieve:
Because thy promise I believe,

Just as I am (thy love unknown
Has broken every barrier down),
Now to be thine, yea, thine alone,

Just as I am, of that free love,
The breadth, length, depth, and height to prove,
Here for a season, then above.

Psalm 96 *Cantate Domino*

1 Sing to the Lord a new song; * sing to the Lord, all the earth.

2 Sing to the Lord and bless his name; * tell out his salvation from day to day.

3 Declare his glory among the nations * and his wonders among all peoples.

4 For great is the Lord and greatly to be praised; * he is more to be feared than all gods.

5 For all the gods of the nations are but idols; * it is the Lord who made the heavens.

6 Honour and majesty are before him; *
power and splendour are in his sanctuary!

7 Ascribe to the Lord, you families of the peoples; * ascribe to the Lord honour and strength.

8 Ascribe to the Lord the honour due to his name; *
bring offerings and come into his courts.

9 O worship the Lord in the beauty of holiness; * let the whole earth tremble before him.

10 Tell it out among the nations that the Lord is king. *
He has made the world so firm that it cannot be moved; he will judge the peoples with equity.

Glory ...

O come to the waters, everyone who thirsts; and you that have no money, come, buy wine and milk without money and without price. Why do you spend your money for that which is not bread, and your labour for that which does not satisfy? Listen carefully to me, and eat what is good, and delight yourselves in rich food. Incline your ear, and come to me; listen that you may live. I will make with you an everlasting covenant, my steadfast, sure love for David.

(Isaiah 55:1-3)

Jesus Christ is the same yesterday and today and forever. Let us then go to him outside the camp and bear the abuse he endured. For here we have no lasting city, but we are looking for the city that is to come. Through him, then, let us continually offer a sacrifice of praise to God, that is, the fruit of lips that confess his name. Do not neglect to do good and to share what you have, for such sacrifices are pleasing to God.

(Hebrews 13:8,13-16)

Jesus said to the Jews, 'I am the bread of life. Whoever comes to me will never be hungry, and whoever believes in me will never be thirsty. And this is the will of him who sent me, that I should lose nothing of all that he has given me, but raise it up on the last day. This is indeed the will of my Father, that all who see the Son and believe in him may have eternal life; and I will raise them up on the last day.'

(John 6:35,39-40)

The Gospel Canticle
+ My soul proclaims the greatness of the Lord ... (see p. 169)

Intercessions
- That we may realise our priesthood in offering the sacrifice of praise ...
- That we may value the gifts of creation as sacraments of God's love ...
- That we may learn in worship to look for the Lord's coming again ...

Our Father ...

Build in our hearts, O God, a holy Temple,
wherein to adore you, our Father,
to give thanks to Jesus, our Redeemer,
and to welcome your Holy Spirit,
so that the brightness of your Presence
may shine within us and through us,
to the glory of your Name. *Amen.*

Lord,
let my prayer be set forth
in thy sight as the incense;
and let the lifting up of my hands
be an evening sacrifice
now and always. *Amen.*

+ The grace of our Lord Jesus Christ, and the love of God, and the
fellowship of the Holy Spirit be with us all, evermore. *Amen.*

Friday

+ O God, make speed to save us.
O Lord, make haste to help us.
Glory be ...   Alleluia   *(except in Lent)*

Abide with me; fast falls the eventide;
The darkness deepens; Lord with me abide!
When other helpers fail, and comforts flee,
Help of the helpless, O abide with me.

I need thy presence every passing hour;
What but thy grace can foil the tempter's power?
Who like thyself my guide and stay can be?
Through cloud and sunshine, O abide with me.

I fear no foe with thee at hand to bless;
Ills have no weight, and tears no bitterness.
Where is death's sting? where, grave, thy victory?
I triumph still, if thou abide with me.

Hold thou thy Cross before my closing eyes;
Shine through the gloom, and point me to the skies:
Heaven's morning breaks, and earth's vain shadows flee;
In life, in death, O Lord, abide with me!

Psalm 102   *Domine, exaudi*

1 O Lord, hear my prayer *
   and let my crying come before you.

2 Hide not your face from me * in the day of my distress.

3 Incline your ear to me; *
   when I call, make haste to answer me,

4 For my days are consumed in smoke, *
   and my bones burn away as in a furnace.

5 My heart is smitten down and withered like grass, *
   so that I forget to eat my bread.

6 From the sound of my groaning *
   my bones cleave fast to my skin.

13 But you, O Lord, shall endure for ever, *
   and your name through all generations.

14 You will arise and have pity on Zion, * it is time to have mercy
   upon her; surely the time has come.

15 For your servants love her very stones, *
   and feel compassion for her dust.

16 Then shall the nations fear your name, O Lord, *
   and all the kings of the earth your glory.

Glory ...

Sion said, 'The Lord has forsaken me, my Lord has forgotten me.' Can a woman forget her nursing child, or show no compassion for the child of her womb? Even if these may forget, yet I will never forget you. See, I have engraved you on the palms of my hands; your walls are continually before me. (Isaiah 49:14-16)

In all these things we are more than conquerors through him who loved us. For I am convinced that neither death, nor life, nor angels, nor rulers, nor things present, nor things to come, nor powers, nor height, nor depth, nor anything else in all creation, will be able to separate us from the love of God in Christ Jesus our Lord. (Romans 8:37-39)

Jesus said to Philip and Andrew, 'Very truly, I tell you, unless a grain of wheat falls into the earth and dies, it remains just a single grain; but if it dies, it bears much fruit. Those who love their life lose it, and those who hate their life in this world will keep it for eternal life. Whoever serves me must follow me, and where I am, there will my servant be also. Whoever serves me, the Father will honour.' (John 12:24-26)

The Gospel Canticle
+ My soul proclaims the greatness of the Lord ... (see p. 169)

Intercessions
- For the courage to name falsehood and evil ...
- That those in authority might use their power wisely for the good of all ...
- For all who are nearing death, and those who wait with them ...
Our Father ...

Almighty Father,
look with mercy on this your family
for which our Lord Jesus Christ
was content to be betrayed,
given up into the hands of sinners
and suffer death upon the cross,
who is alive and reigns with you
and the Holy Spirit,
one God, now and for ever. *Amen.*

Prevent us, O Lord, in all our doings
with thy most gracious favour,
and further us with thy continual help;
that in all our works begun, continued,
and ended in thee, we may glorify thy holy name,
and finally by thy mercy obtain everlasting life. *Amen.*

+ The grace of our Lord Jesus Christ, and the love of God, and the fellowship of the Holy Spirit be with us all, evermore. *Amen.*

Saturday

+ O God, make speed to save us.
O Lord, make haste to help us.

Glory ...   Alleluia (except in Lent)

Praise to the Holiest in the height
And in the depth be praise,
In all his words most wonderful,
Most sure in all his ways.

O loving wisdom of our God!
When all was sin and shame,
A second Adam to the fight
And to the rescue came.

O generous love! that he who smote
In Man for man the foe,
The double agony in Man
For man should undergo;

And in the garden secretly,
And on the Cross on high,
Should teach his brethren, and inspire
To suffer and to die.

Praise to the Holiest in the height,
And in the depth be praise,
In all his words most wonderful,
Most sure in all his ways.

Psalm 130   *De profundis*

1 Out of the depths have I cried to you,
   O Lord; Lord, hear my voice;*
   let your ears consider well the voice of my supplication.

2 If you, Lord, were to mark what is done amiss, * O Lord, who
   could stand?

3 But there is forgiveness with you; * so that you shall be feared.

4 I wait for the Lord; my soul waits for him; * in his word is my
   hope.

5 My soul waits for the Lord,
   more than the night-watch for the morning, * more than the
   night-watch for the morning.

6 O Israel, wait for the Lord, *
   for with the Lord there is mercy;

7 With him is plenteous redemption, *
   and he shall redeem Israel from all their sins.

Glory ...

Scripture reading

See, I am sending my messenger to prepare the way before me,
and the Lord whom you seek will suddenly come to his temple.
The messenger of the covenant in whom you delight – indeed, he
is coming, says the Lord of hosts. But who can endure the day of
his coming, and who can stand when he appears? (Malachi 3:1-3)

I consider that the sufferings of this present time are not worth
comparing with the glory about to be revealed to us. For the
creation waits with eager longing for the revealing of the children
of God; for the creation was subjected to futility, not of its own
will but by the will of one who subjected it, in hope that the
creation itself would be set free from its bondage to decay and
obtain the freedom of the glory of the children of God.

(Romans 8:18-21)

When Jesus came to the place, he looked up and said to Zacchaeus,
'Zacchaeus, hurry and come down; for I must stay at your house
today.' Zacchaeus stood there and said to the Lord, 'Look, half of
my possessions, Lord, I will give to the poor; and if I have
defrauded anyone of anything, I will pay back four times as much.'
Then Jesus said to him, 'Today salvation has come to this house,
because he too is a son of Abraham. For the Son of Man came to
seek out and to save the lost.' (Luke 19:5,8-10)

The Gospel Canticle
+ My soul proclaims the greatness of the Lord ... (see p. 169)

Intercessions
• That we may have faith in the reality of the life beyond the grave ...
• That with ready hearts and clean consciences we may worship the Lord ...
• That we may stand with confidence on the day of judgement ...

Our Father ...

Abide with us, Lord, for it is toward evening
and the day is far spent;
abide with us and with your whole Church.
Abide with us in the evening of the day,
in the evening of life,
in the evening of the world.
Abide with us and with all your faithful ones,
O Lord, in time and eternity. *Amen.*

As watchmen look for the morning,
so do we look for thee, O Christ.
Come with the dawning of day,
and make yourself known to us
in the breaking of bread;
for thou art our God,
for ever and ever. *Amen.*

+ The grace of our Lord Jesus Christ, and the love of God, and the fellowship of the Holy Spirit be with us all, evermore. *Amen.*